CHRISTIAN LOVE AND SELF-DENIAL

An Historical and Normative Study of Jonathan Edwards, Samuel Hopkins, and American Theological Ethics

Stephen G. Post, Ph.D.

UNIVERSITY
PRESS OF
AMERICA

LANHAM • NEW YORK • LONDON

Copyright © 1987 by

University Press of America,® Inc.

4720 Boston Way
Lanham, MD 20706

3 Henrietta Street
London WC2E 8LU England

Printed in the United States of America

British Cataloging in Publication Information Available

Library of Congress Cataloging in Publication Data

Post, Stephen Garrard, 1951-
    Christian love and self-denial.

    Bibliography: p.
    Includes index.
    1. Edwards, Jonathan, 1745-1801—Contributions in
theology of love.   2. Hopkins, Samuel, 1721-1803—
Contributions in theology of love.   3. Love (Theology)—
History of doctrines—18th century.   4. Self-denial—
History of doctrines—18th century.   5. Christian
ethics—History—18th century.   I. Title.
BV4639.E359P67   1987   241'.4   86-28147
ISBN 0-8191-5261-7 (alk. paper)
ISBN 0-8191-5262-5 (pbk. : alk. paper)

All University Press of America books are produced on acid-free
paper which exceeds the minimum standards set by the National
Historical Publication and Records Commission.

So far goes asceticism in the New Testament. It does not go far enough to take a man out of human society or to annihilate the natural impulses with which God endowed him.

Walter Rauschenbusch, The Righteousness of the Kingdom

Christian altruism never takes the form of saying, "I myself ought to be or become nothing; while others only are to be served and saved." For God who loves me demands not that I should be nothing, but that I should be his own.

Josiah Royce, The Problem of Christianity

Love to God. Self-love. Whether or no a man ought to love God more than himself. Self-love, taken in its most extensive sense, love to God, are not things properly capable of being compared with one another; for they are not opposites or things entirely distinct, but one enters into the nature of the other.

Jonathan Edwards, Miscellany 530

TABLE OF CONTENTS

Introduction

This is an historical and normative study in the field of American theological ethics. It details an important debate within early American Protestantism over the form and meaning of Christian love. In particular, it focuses on the thought of Jonathan Edwards and Samuel Hopkins, who differed markedly on the question of whether all self-love is prohibited from Christian ethics. The origins of this debate are shown to lie in a basic divergence of opinion as to the degree of self-denial theocentric piety demands — a divergence which loomed large among the Puritans. A normative discussion of this debate is then developed primarily with reference to contemporary American theological ethicists who have borrowed from the Edwardsean materials.

The significance of Samuel Hopkins' thought has often been overlooked by those interested in American religious ethics. Hopkins, however, is an important figure. He entered Yale University in 1737, and served as a Congregational minister first in Great Barrington, Massachusetts (1743-1769), and then in Newport, until his death in 1803. Hopkins was a student of Edwards, and an ardent admirer of Mrs. Sarah Pierpont Edwards, Jonathan's wife. In contrast to Edwards, Hopkins argued that the test of Christian love is absolute disinterest in one's own well-being. William Ellery Channing, the leader of nineteenth-century Unitarianism, wrote of Hopkins: "True virtue, as he taught, was an entire surrender of personal interest to the benevolent purposes of God. Self-love he spared in none of its movements.[1]

From Hopkins, American Protestantism was bequeathed a doctrine of radically self-denying love which had significant impact.[2] During the period of the Second Great Awakening, America's first foreign missionaries, inspired by Hopkins' theology of love, braved the perils of spreading the Gospel in unknown regions of the world; and various participants in the earliest anti-slavery movements looked back to Hopkins as their theological source. Central to this study is Hopkins' doctrine of "disinterested benevolence," arguably one of the more significant theories of Christian love in American Protestant history insofar as it informed many of the benevolence associations of the early Nineteenth Century — associations so prominent that they were dubbed the "Benevolent Empire" and inspired Alexis deToqueville's observations on religion and the Republic.[3] Without overstating the case for Hopkins, suffice it to conclude that his theological ethic is not one to be ignored.

To some extent, Hopkins was an infamous figure, made so by his insistence that the last iota of self-love to be driven from the Christian breast. The Christian must, he insisted, be "willing to be damned for the glory of God" before his or her love is worthy. The famous challenge of Hopkins, "Are you willing to be damned for the glory of God?" became the standard test for Congregationalist candidates for the ministry during the Second Great Awakening. Hopkins could countenance no compromise with self-love in any of its forms, for as he put it, love of self is nothing but "a wild beast waiting to be uncaged." Christian love, for Hopkins, meant self-denial without limits.

Had Jonathan Edwards not died in his intellectual prime, he might well have taken the time to correct the excesses of his esteemed student Hopkins. Edwards' ideal of Christian love was one inclusive of a form of self-love, such that the notion of the Christian surrendering participation in the mutual good appalled him. Certainly Edwards advocated a theocentric piety which would enable the self to transcend egoism and join in the harmonious "consent of being to being," but he placed clear limits on the degree to which Christian ethics should preach self-denial and he had no tolerance at all for the test of willing one's own damnation which Hopkins popularized. Edwards did not confuse the genuine Christian ideal of unselfishness with the false ideal of selflessness for a number of reasons: First, he clearly stood in line with the intellectual heritage of his maternal grandfather, Solomon Stoddard, an orthodox Puritan in his suspicion of the extreme renunciation of the natural inclination towards well-being and happiness; second, during the course of the Northampton revivals, Edwards was distressed by a suicide which he ascribed to melancholy and the piety of radical resignation characterized by "the willingness to be damned" that has established itself in New England during his period; third, he was convinced on empirical grounds that the self always seeks happiness such that the ideal of total self-denial struck him as an abstraction divorced from concrete human experience; fourth, Edwards was certain that Scripture promises true happiness to the saint, and therefore works with human nature rather than against it; and finally, he viewed God as the exemplar of perfect happiness due to the mutual love between Father and Son, and he himself felt the overflow of this divine joy as communicated

ix

through the Spirit in conversion experience. Of course Edwards was careful to proscribe selfishness and forms of self-love concerned with one's own well-being for its own sake independent of community. But true self-love, i.e., "consent" to one's own being in fellowship with God and neighbor, he did not deny.

The first chapter of this book focuses on one source of the ideal of radically self-denying love in Christian ethics generally. It contrasts the Augustinian tradition of ethical ideas with the ideal of "pure" love. True self-love, argued Augustine, is co-extensive with the self's love for God. Though theoretically distinct, these two ethical-religious mandates require the same action. As the self's Highest Good, there is no love for God which does not satisfy the desire for happiness; similarly, there is not true happiness without love for God. This Augustinian strain was unquestioned until the twelfth century, when figures in the tradition began to doubt its adequacy. God should be loved, they argued, without any thought of even true happiness and well-being, for Christian love "seeketh not its own." Finally, this effort to drive a wedge between love for God and all self-love became a matter of broad popular concern in the seventeenth-century "pure love controversy" in France. Madame Guyon and Francois de Fénelon contended that "pure love" transcends the desire for happiness, and must be tested by the hypothetical acceptance of eternal damnation. "If God throws you to eternal misery," asked Fénelon, "in this case, will you still love him?" The position of pure or disinterested love spread into German Pietist circles, the English revival of John Wesley, and elsewhere. However, this ideal of resignation did not continue unchallenged. Within British Puritanism, a number of theologians known collectively as the

"British Augustinians" consciously incorporated Augustinian themes into Puritan thought. William Perkins and William Ames are foremost in this group, along with Thomas Watson and others. Jonathan Edwards drew on Ames in particular, and carefully stayed within the bounds of Puritan Augustinian thought while allowing some room for disinterested love. In essence, this means that Edwards' theology of love is indebted to these figures insofar as he consistently affirmed that God works with, not against, true self-love.

However, the piety and theology of pure love made gains among the New England Puritans, as evidenced by the fact that Samuel Willard of Boston devoted his late seventeenth-century treatise to a refutation of those who would divide Christian ethics from self-love in all its forms. It is not my intent to make a strong claim regarding direct historical connections between the European "pure love controversy" and Puritan theology, for the evidence is quite slim; suffice it to note that the medieval doctrine of radical resignation (resignatio ad infernum) had its parallel among the New England Puritans. Indeed, the notion of "the willingness to be damned" was a matter of public controversy, for otherwise Willard would not have deemed it worthy of refutation. This New England controversy is discussed in Chapter Two.

The ethics of Edwards and Hopkins are best understood with this controversy in mind, for the degree to which love for God demands self-denial informs the extent to which the Christian is obligated to sacrifice for the neighbor. If limits are placed on self-denial before God, then mutuality or communion can more readily emerge as the ideal of Christian love. Thus, the Augustinian Edwards insisted that, "Love in heaven is always mutual."[4] Selfless love for God of the sort proposed by

Hopkins fails to recognize that the structure of personal and social existence requires a theology of love that allows for the self to participate in the good of communion.

Some theological ethicists will question the attention given to the nature of theocentric piety and love for God in the first chapter, as well as in the second, which focuses on American Puritan thinkers in detail, because they overlook the relation between piety and ethics. What does the "religious" problem of love for God have to do with the "ethical" one of human interrelations? I can only refer the reader to the writings of James M. Gustafson, who argues that ethics in the American theocentric context begins with piety before a sovereign God which makes the self-denial ethical life requires possible. "A theocentric piety," writes Gustafson, "I believe, motivates and issues in a readiness to restrain particular interests for the sake of other persons, for communities, and the larger world."[5] He adds, incidentally, that one "does not have to be willing to be damned for the glory of God to be moved to forms of self-giving toward others ..."[6] Here Gustafson is in accord with Edwards.

Jonathan Edwards, the focus of my third chapter, sets limits to self-denial for a number of reasons, all of which I examine in detail. In addition, the various themes in Edwards' thought which point in the direction of communion as the ideal of Christian love are highlighted. The fourth chapter deals exclusively with the theology of Samuel Hopkins. It must be acknowledged that another student of Edwards, Joseph Bellamy (d. 1790) argued for the separation of Christian love from any element of self-love. Bellamy too advocated the test of willing one's damnation in order to assure the purity of love. Hopkins, however, went far beyond Bellamy in emphasizing the heights of disinterestedness, so it is on his writings that I concentrate.

In the fifth and final chapter, I turn to a normative assessment of the American Protestant debate over Christian love and self-denial. In particular, I critically assess certain themes from Edwards and, though to a lesser extent, Hopkins, which have been developed to set one framework for debate among contemporary American Christian ethicists. I also offer a number of constructive suggestions with regard to the theology of love which are related to these themes.

I would like to thank the National Endowment for the Humanities, which provided me with a Summer Fellowship for Independent Research to write this text. In addition, I am grateful to the Society of Christian Ethics for inviting me to present the third chapter at the 1985 annual meeting, as well as to the Journal of Religious Ethics, which published some of my material on Edwards and Hopkins in the Fall of 1986 under the title, "Disinterested Benevolence: An American Debate Over the Nature of Christian Love." Professors James M. Gustafson, Robin W. Lovin, and Jerald C. Brauer of the University of Chicago Divinity School are to be gratefully credited with supervising my doctoral dissertation, out of which certain of the themes in this book were later developed. Credit is also due to the Institute for the Advanced Study of Religion at the Divinity School, where I began to write on the theme of Christian love as a Junior Fellow in 1983. Finally, a note of appreciation is due the William Clemons Library at the University of Michigan in Ann Arbor, where most of this book was written, as well as to Robert Leisy for editorial assistance.

xiii

Footnotes

1. William Ellery Channing, D.D., Works (Boston: American Unitarian Association, 1892), p. 424.

2. Hopkins also contributed to the theme of American millenialism. See Joseph A. Conforti, Samuel Hopkins and the New Divinity Movement (Grand Rapids, Michigan: Wm. B. Eerdsmans Publishing Company, 1981); also Ernest Lee Tuveson, Redeemer Nation: The Idea of America's Millennial Role (Chicago: University of Chicago Midway Reprint, 1968).

3. See Alexis deTocqueville, Democracy in America (New York: Vintage Books, 1945), vol. 1, ch. 17, "Principle Causes Which Tend to Maintain the Democratic Republic in the United States."

4. Jonathan Edwards, Charity And Its Fruits (London: Banner of Truth Press, 1978), p. 338.

5. James M. Gustafson, Ethics From a Theocentric Perspective: Ethics and Theology (Chicago: University of Chicago Press, 1984), 2:22.

6. Ibid.

Chapter I

Love For God And Self-Denial

What degree of self-denial does love for God require? That God is to be loved is clear from the first half of the love commandment, "Love the Lord your God with all your heart, and all your soul, and all your mind" (Matt. 22:37-38; also Mark 12:31 and Luke 10:27). But must even the last iota of self-love be cast aside in order to make this love for God truly worthy?

To contend that it is in the relation of the person to God that a perspective on self-love and the impropriety of undue self-assertion emerges seems to me a reasonable point of departure for Christian ethics.[1] Resignation before the sovereignty of God passes over into human relations in the form of humility and other-regarding affections. But are there limits to the resignation of self that love for God requires? What limits can be established will inform the character of human interaction. If there are no limits, then resignation before God often translates into unconstrained self-denial before one's neighbor. This is evident in the thought of Hopkins in particular. To be "willing to be damned for the Glory of God," meant a selflessness in human relations that went far beyond Edwards' call

1

for mere unselfishness.

Historically, the ideal of radical self-denying love for God in New England theology parallels that of the mystics of the seventeenth century. As one scholar has noted, "This absolute renunciation of the ordinary ties and preferences of the self for the sake of the Highest Love was with Madame Guyon, as well as with others of the period, part of an overmastering and deeply interesting impulse which swept over Europe in the latter part of the seventeenth century."[2] This is not to suggest that the French pure-love mystics such as Guyon were read by Puritans, but only that the impulse towards radical self-denial evident in their writings is indicative of a trend during this period which, though difficult to explain, was very widespread. It is fair to claim, for instance, that the spirituality of Mrs. Sarah Pierpont Edwards, Jonathan's wife, resonates with that of Guyon. There is no direct relationship between the two women, and yet the similarities with regard to an uncompromising stress on the heights of self-denial are striking.

That the American experience and the European controversy over pure love and self-denial may be directly related is best evidenced in the writings of Cotton Mather. French Catholic advocates of pure love for God, such as Fénelon and Guyon, as well as the Spanish mystic Molinos, had, in the words of Richard F. Lovelace, "a great deal of influence on Franke and Halle Pietism."[3] Mather was in constant communication by letter with the Pietists, and developed a doctrine of self-abnegating love for God "showing affinities for Jansenism and Quietism."[4] Rearticulating the medieval mystic notion of resignatio ad infernum, or the willingness to love God even if one is cast into damnation, Mather wrote that if God should "cast me off," still, "I will adore Him, and forever silence all murmuring against Him!"[5] Furthermore, Mather refers favorably to Fénelon in several of his writings.[6]

2

Mather, then, was not insulated from the European debates over love and self-denial. In addition, Edwards, as Norman Fiering mentions, was himself familiar later in his career with the writings of Fénelon's English convert to Catholicism and radically disinterested love, the "Chevalier" Andrew Michael Ramsey.[7] Moreover, any American moralist aware of Lord Shaftesbury's moral sense theories might have been cognizant of the latter's reference to "the pious, worthy, and ingenious Abbe Fénelon."[8] So it can be guardedly suggested that certain New England theologians were aware of the European concern with pure or fully disinterested love as an alternative to its Augustinian or eudaemonistic antithesis. However, clearer evidence of this awareness is lacking, such that it can only be firmly argued that there existed a parallel New England concern. This chapter focuses on the debate over self-denial and love for God as it emerged in the wider historical tradition of Christian thought and converged on New England theology.

The Augustinian Position

Augustine placed limits on the piety of self-denial by appropriating the Greek notion of well-being or eudaemonism into the Christian framework. The Christian ethic does not run counter to the proper love of self, but rather redirects the self towards the object of true happiness. Christians, he argued, "do not strive to destroy themselves ... ."[9] "Following after God is the desire for happiness; to reach God is happiness itself," he concluded.[10] "All men," he declared, "desire to live happily."[11] Happiness is achieved when "that which is man's chief end is both loved and possessed."[12]

Though theoretically distinct, love for God and true well-being entail the same ethical action. Without love for God, there can be no true love of self, for God is the natural end of the self who alone brings persons to fulfillment.

Augustine, then, had no interest in placing a barrier between Christian love for God and proper self-love. Indeed, he was suspicious of the notion of utter self-denial in much the same way Edwards was, since both thinkers were concerned with the delicate line between sacrifice and a melancholic inability to establish the appropriate form of self-regard. As John Burnaby has written, "For Augustine, the question of 'disinterestedness' never arose at all. Pure love, castus amor, is the desire of God only, but it is the desire of God."[13] The idea of radical resignation to the point of "holy indifference" to one's own well-being had no place in Augustine's thought.

The self-love Augustine insists on, then, is not a self-referring duty independent of love for God. Yet it is still self-love, which is why Augustine avoids a piety in which all thought of the self is denied. Oliver O'Donovan has stated the Augustinian position succinctly:

> On the one hand, self-love might be represented as an area of self-referring duty independent of and complementary to the love of God. . . . On the other hand, love of God might be represented as a spirit of devotion from which, at the highest moments, all thought of self is strained out, a position maintained by the medieval champions of "pure" love. But Augustine has no place either for a virtue of self-love independent of love for God or the love of God without self-love.[14]

The self, according to Augustine, is never free of desire; the point is that it should turn towards the

4

one thing truly worth desiring.

The Augustinian view of the self and its implications for the meaning of Christian love held sway over Western thought largely without resistance until the twelfth century, when the love theme "occupied the attention of thoughtful and creative men and women as it did in no other medieval century."[15] Gradually an alternative view emerged. But still, Augustinianism would be maintained as the dominant tradition. Thus William of St. Thierry (d. 1147) restated the Augustinian position as follows:

> In fact, love is a power of the soul, leading her by a kind of natural gravity to her place of destination. Every creature, whether spiritual or corporeal, has both a place to which it is naturally led and a kind of gravity by which it is led there.[16]

The phrase "naturally led and a kind of gravity by which it is led there" is typically Augustinian insofar as the basic tendencies of the self figure so prominently in the definition of love William puts forward. Another Augustinian, the Cistercian Aelred of Rivaulx (d. 1167) wrote the following: "From the moment if creation, man was . . . given a capacity for happiness."[17] Noteworthy here is the appreciation on Aelred's part for the order of nature as created with certain capacities which are not to be ignored in articulating the definition of love. The Augustinian assumption that God has created the soul restless and in need so that it might turn and adhere to God for its own true good informs Aelred's thought, as it did that of Thomas Aquinas.

While true happiness and true self-love, the result of communion with God, are wholly justified by the Augustinians, there is a powerful Augustinian proscription against loving God for the sake of "external" goods (goods other than God), i.e., to look for a reward other than God and communion with God, for this is to love not God, but the supposed reward, and is thus an attempt to manipulate God for one's own selfish ends. True self-love and selfishness are thus clearly distinguished.

Alas, not all could be satisfied with the admission of self-love into the Christian ethic. There arose a new strain in the tradition advocating a form of love which leaves all self-love and hope behind. It is a strain which confuses selflessness with the virtue of unselfish love, ignores the structures of human nature, draws from a questionable theology of the cross, and makes an ideal of unlimited resignation with no adequate appreciation of the theological virtue of hope.

The Pure or Disinterested Alternative

Pure love theorists discarded the metaphysical view that all beings seek their own good. All but the love that "seeketh not its own" is deemed unworthy because it is tainted with impurity and egoism. To love God so purely means that the sort of language used by an Augustinian such as Edwards to describe God — the "sweet" to be relished — is no longer appropriate. Any ethic which insists on radical self-denial before God can hardly allow for such expressions of joy.

The test for pure love is not communion and true happiness, but disinterestedness or indifference. From Abelard to Fénelon and Hopkins, imaginative tests were devised to make certain that Christian love is free from the least admixture with self-love. Indeed, tests such as the "willingness to be damned" were intended to assure an indifference to personal well-being.

The emergence of pure love may owe much to Abelard (d. 1142). Paul L. Williams contrasts Abelard's thought with that of Augustine as

follows: "Perhaps the striking originality of
Abelard's doctrine can be seen in its opposition to
the views of St. Augustine.   Augustine could not
conceive of a love for God which denied all interest
in divine beatitude."[18]   Abelard did write that it is
selfish to love God because God loves us.   Rather,
God should be loved "no matter what He does to
me."   Dissatisfied with the Augustinian ethic,
Abelard apparently moved in the direction of
radically self-denying love, though at various points
in his writings he too allowed for the Augustinian
distinction between selfishness and true self-love.

Abelard's suspicion of all love of self, if we are to
believe Etiénne Gilson, may be related to the
relationship between Abelard and Heloise, one of
pure love insofar as the latter gave up the joyful
possibility of marital union and yet loved Abelard
still.   Heloise detached herself from the happiness
which marriage to her beloved would have
brought.   In his analysis of the letters of Heloise and
Abelard, Gilson highlights the theme of "absolute
disinterestedness" which the letters emphasize.[19]
The ideal of a completely pure love which
anticipates no response from the beloved "deeply
impressed" subsequent thinking on love for God.[20]

Thus in the wake of the twelfth century, we find
Duns Scotus (d. 1309) distinguishing the "natural"
pole of the human will that seeks God out of need
as the Summum Bonum, from the "free" pole
which is capable of disinterested love independent
of the tendency towards well-being.   Allen B.
Wolter interprets this distinction as indication that
Scotus was moving away from the metaphysical
assumptions underlying the more traditional
eudaemonistic framework:

> But Scotus saw a still more basic freedom
> in will, one that Aristotle failed to recognize.
> Their (the Aristotelian's) theory of man's
> appetites and loves can be called physical in
> the original sense of the term.   All striving,

all activity, stems from an imperfection in the agent, whose actions all tend to complete its nature . . . . Since what perfects a thing is its good, and since striving for what is good is a form of love, we could say that all activity is sparked by love. The peculiarity of such love however is that it can never be truly altruistic or even objective. It is radically self-centered in the sense that nature seeks primarily and above all else its own welfare.[21]

The "free" pole of the will is, argued Scotus, capable of love without seeking the good of the lover. It lies beyond the pale of natural seeking. This pole of the will is free of the metaphysical finality of other natural causes, acting from a liberty of indifference to well-being and of spontaneity.

To some extent, Scotus' dissatisfaction with the Augustinian position may be attributable to Franciscan influence, for like some others in the Franciscan tradition, Scotus departed from the eudaemonistic presuppositions of earlier figures in the Christian heritage. Yet it is a mistake to generalize here regarding the Franciscans', for Bonaventure held decidedly Augustinian views. As John Burnaby has pointed out, Scotus himself, at any rate, was at odds with the views of Thomas Aquinas in this regard: "Against the endeavor of St. Thomas to justify and safeguard from abuse the eudaemonist form which Christian ethics has received from Augustine, the work of Duns Scotus stands out as a resolute refusal to compromise. Amor Concupiscentia is to have no place in the love which fulfills the first great commandment. Self-interest must be wholly excluded, and this can only be if in the last resort the self can cease to will even its own being."[22] But it is just this radical exclusion of all self-love from the ethical life that appears highly ambiguous.

Another figure who takes up the banner of

selfless love is Meister Eckhart (d. 1328). He considerably developed an idea which would have lasting impact on Western thought about love — the idea of "disinterest." "Pure disinterest is empty nothingness," wrote Eckhart.[23] Moreover, "The disinterested person, . . . wants nothing, and neither has he anything of which he would be rid."[24] Without going into an analysis of Eckhart's thought, suffice it only to mention that the ideal of selflessness and disinterested love is developed in his work, although an Augustinian appreciation for true self-love is not entirely lost.

Coupled with Scotus' suspicions of the Augustinian position, Eckhart's views would influence the Protestant Reformation. The traditional Catholic teleological ethics which so cherished the hope of personal well-being gave way to a thoroughly obediential form of love. The rule of God replaced the beatific vision.

The ground, then, had been prepared for Martin Luther to make a statement which de-emphasizes the natural strivings of the human soul and reduces the role of self-love in Christian ethics: "Blessedness is this, to will the will of God and His glory in all things, and to desire nothing of one's own either in this world or the next."[25] The revolt against a teleological notion of love thus became embedded in Lutheran theology.

Karl Holl writes that Luther rejected the medieval concept of love which "received its standard from Augustine," and was rooted in "the quest for happiness" or the "eudaemonistic conception of the moral law." According to Holl, Luther understood the Augustinian notion of love as incompatible with "truly selfless love, that is, one that renounces one's own happiness for God's sake . . . ."[26] Another of Luther's interpreters, Wilhelm Pauck, argues that Luther totally rejected the eudaemonistic ethical framework: "Luther calls this way of loving God through which men seek eternal

9

bliss <u>amor concupiscentiae</u>, i.e., a covetous or selfish love."[27]   Finally, there is George W. Forrell's remark as follows: "Against this prudential conception of love which has been developed even further by scholasticism, Luther placed what he considered the 'biblical' conception of love. According to Luther, Christian love is diametrically opposed to all human acquisitive desire."[28]

That Luther departed from Augustinianism is generally agreed on.   Luther inherited and developed the indictment of self-love characteristic of Duns Scotus and Eckhart.   Contemporary Lutheran ethicists such as Anders Nygren, who insists on driving the wedge between agape and all self-love, make self-denial the central defining feature of Christian love and thus follow Luther's anti-Augustinianism.   This constitutes a major difficulty for Christian ethics, for it removes Christian love from the structure of human nature as the Augustinians defined it.   Criticism of this Lutheran influence on American theological ethics will await later treatment.   For the moment, it is sufficient to note James Luther Adams' remark that Nygren's separation of agape from all eros amounts to a "mere Lutheran tract."[29]

It is especially important, given that the focus of this book is on the American tradition, to turn attention to the thought of Calvin.   Samuel Hopkins, after all, described himself as a "consistent Calvinist," and consistent he was.   In developing an ethic of radical self-denial, Hopkins and the Hopkinsians carried Calvinist theology to an extreme.   Calvinism, as Hopkins viewed it, would have no quarrel with the seventeenth-century impulse in European piety and mysticism to jettison self-love entirely.

Calvin put the sovereignty of God in the center of his thought, and stressed obedience to God's will. When Cardinal Sadoleto, Catholic Bishop of Geneva, told his lost parishioners to reject the new

Calvinist faith, because Catholicism offers a more certain path to salvation, Calvin "retorted that man should not be so preoccupied with his salvation."[30] Calvin argued, claims Roland Bainton, that "the chief end of man is not to save himself or to be assured that he is saved, but to honor God."[31] The Augustinian emphasis on true self-love and well-being is replaced by a nonteleological abandonment to God's will.

Calvin did indeed attempt to remove most self-love from the Christian ethic. "We are not our own: insofar as we can, let us therefore forget ourselves and all that is ours," he wrote.[32] God's decrees are "unsearchable" or beyond human understanding; it is, moreover, vain to fight against them. In any case, each person is already saved or damned, so worry will make no difference. Though there are other aspects to Calvin's thought that may indicate qualifications on this theme of radical self-abandonment, in basic thrust concern for self has been moved to the periphery of Christian life. As Karl Barth has phrased it, the desire for well-being and salvation is de-emphasized to make central "the signal privilege of serving the Lord."[33] It comes as no surprise, then, that Hopkins and his followers would test candidates for the ministry with the question of their willingness to be damned for the glory of God, in order to root out the last elements of self-love. An ethic of extreme resignation developed in Puritan American circles, then, in part because of an effort to retrieve Calvinism in all its purity. This was at least one element of Hopkins' agenda.

In addition to Reformation Protestant thought, the renunciation of the Augustinian position is characteristic of a strain of seventeenth-century Counter-Reformation Catholicism as well. The Spanish mystic Juan Falconi (d.1638) wrote of the virtue in "utter resignation of His holy will," and was followed by another Spaniard, Miguel de

11

Molinos. Molinos called for a resignation and indifference that is stoic temper far outdid the Stoic ancients. The soul must annihilate all inclinations, even spiritual ones. Self is abolished in perfect pure love for God. Madame Guyon, an adherent in France of Molinos' views, created tremendous division within Catholic circles and beyond. Pure love, she contended, counts no cost, seeks no return, desires nothing, and finds perfect joy in self-giving. It is indifferent to its salvation or damnation, but only obeys, gives, and loses itself without question. There is, she argued, "never enough of disinterestedness." In the 1690's Guyon was denounced by Jacques Bossuet, bishop of Meaux, in his effort to reaffirm the Augustinian notion that love is grounded in nature and seeks the good.

It was Fénelon who came to Guyon's defense. Evelyn Underhill, a modern authority on mysticism, writes that Fénelon's widely published letters of spiritual direction "reached and affected the eighteenth-century Quakers, the leaders of the Evangelical revival, the Tractarians; and in his own country taught and still teaches . . . ."[34] In 1750 Fénelon's Dissertation on Pure Love was published in Germantown, Pennsylvania, and became a mainstay of Quaker spirituality.[35] This historian Austin Warren writes that even earlier the colonies had been familiarized with Fénelon's writings. In a chapter entitled " Fénelon Among the Anglo-Saxons," Warren mentions Jonathan Edwards as the first Congregationalist to introduce the pure-love Quietists into the colonies via the writings of the "Chevalier" Ramsey: "The first theologian who, by knowledge and sympathy, introduced the Quietists into America was Edwards, who a few years before his death, became acquainted with The Philosophical Principles of Natural and Revealed Religion (1747) by Ramsey."[36] This statement should be immediately qualified, for

Edwards had major criticisms of the Quietist's extreme emphasis on self-denying love.

Later, contends Warren, Fénelon would become the principal spiritual guide for the Boston Transcendentalists. So much was this the case that Fénelon's name is incised with the names of W. E. Channing and Theodore Parker, and various other Unitarians and Transcendentalists, on the outer wall of the Boston Public Library.[37] This history underscores the interaction of the later American theologians with the European figures associated with pure love.

Perhaps at no other point in Christian history did the tension between Augustinianism and pure or disinterested love become a matter of wider public concern than in the famous "Querelle du pur amour," which occurred in France between Fénelon and Bossuet. In 1699, Fénelon's views were condemned by Pope Innocent XII. Defending mystics such as Madame Guyon, Fénelon advocated a love for God hypothetically indifferent to both union with the divine and to one's own salvation. Fénelon's views were condemned for what must be accepted as sound reasons: he made folly of the theological virtue of hope; he argued for an indifference to one's own happiness which is a psychological impossibility; and he totally rejected the role of true self-love in Christian ethics.

The British Puritan Augustinians

Before turning to the American Puritan debate over the nature of love as it emerged in the seventeenth and eighteenth centuries, the focus of the following chapter, the impact of the Augustinian position on English Puritanism must be mentioned. There is no better example of the Augustinian influence than William Ames'

13

<u>Marrow of Theology</u> published in 1623.

William Ames was born in 1576 at Ipswich, and was educated at Cambridge, a center of Puritanism. While at Christ's College, Ames studied under William Perkins, who became his close friend. About to be imprisoned for his beliefs, Ames fled England for Holland in 1610, where he encountered, among others, John Robinson. The lectures Ames gave to his students in Leyden between 1620 and 1622 comprise the <u>Marrow</u>. Students at Emmanuel College, Leyden, Harvard and Yale would study the <u>Marrow</u> "as part of basic instruction in divinity," writes one scholar.[38] Moreover, Jonathan Edwards "came into possession of a copy of the 1634 edition in New Haven; he twice signed it and added notes which bespeak his indebtedness."[39]

One feature of Ames' theology is its Augustinianism. Influenced by the work of Perkins, Ames mediated the medieval Augustinian heritage quite consciously and seriously. "We love God in charity because by faith and hope we taste in some measure how good he is . . .," writes Ames.[40] God is the "first good" and we love him "because he has loved us first."[41] Here Ames is quoting 1 John 4:19. "The love which is charity is love of union, of satisfaction or contentment, and good will," maintains the author.[42] In clearly Augustinian terms, Ames concludes thus: "Since our love is a desire of union with God it comes in part from what is called concupiscence or appetite. We desire God ourselves, because we hope for benefit and eternal blessedness from him."[43] The antithesis of love, Ames argues, "is estrangement from God."[44] Just as love is a desire for union so this estrangement is "disjunction," he adds.[45] The desire for union is described as "the inclination of the mind towards God." All of these passages indicate that for Ames, God works with the created aspirations of human nature towards fulfillment and union, rather than against them. As John

Dykstra Eusden has shown recently, the theology of Ames has "Augustinian and scholastic roots."[46] In addition, Ames shows great respect for Thomas Aquinas, leaning heavily on section of <u>Summa Theologica</u>.[47] First, writes Ames, we are to love God, and then ourselves "with the love of true blessedness," only after which are others to be loved such that they not be deprived a blessedness.[48] The notion of a selfless or disinterested love for God simply cannot fit within Ames' theology.

For over a century Ames' <u>Marrow</u> was read by all those aspiring to Puritanism as a clear expression of belief. Its popularity in New England, Holland, and England shows how thoroughly the Augustinian position was established among Puritans. Samuel Willard, to be discussed in the next chapter, was a New England thinker who rook up the task of defending the Augustinian position against those who would drive a wedge between Christian love and all love of self. For as the examination of Willard's text in the next chapter will indicate, by late seventeenth century the idea of a disinterested or pure love had developed in New England, such that Puritan Augustinianism no longer held full sway.

FOOTNOTES

1. See James M. Gustafson, Ethics From a Theocentric Perspective, 2 vols. (Chicago: University of Chicago Press, 1981 and 1984).

2. William C. Piercy, Mysticism in Christianity (New York: Fleming H. Revell Co., 1913), p. 175.

3. Richard F. Lovelace, The American Pietism of Cotton Mather (Wm. B. Eerdmans Publishing Company: Grand Rapids, Michigan, 1979), p.159.

4. Ibid., p. 50.

5. Ibid., p. 159.

6. Lovelace cites letters by Mather describing the French Quietists as "the best Christians," and particularly the "Renowned Chancellor of Paris." Lovelace, p. 159.

7. See Norman Fiering, Jonathan Edwards's Moral Thought in Its British Context (Chapel Hill, North Carolina: University of North Carolina Press, 1981), pp. 172-173.

8. Stanley Grean has written an entire book on Shaftesbury, and emphasizes the impact of Fénelon on his thought. See Grean, Shaftesbury's Philosophy of Religion and Ethics (Ohio: University of Ohio Press, 1967), p. 189.

9. Augustine, On Christian Doctrine, trans. D.W. Robertson, Jr. (New York: Liberal Arts Press, 1958), p. 21.

10. Augustine, The Morals of the Catholic Church, in Whitney J. Oates, trans., Basic Writings of Saint Augustine (New York: Random House, 1948), 1:320.

11. Ibid., 1:321.

12. Ibid., 1:320.

13. John Burnaby, <u>Amor Dei: A Study in the Religion of St. Augustine</u> (London: Hodder & Stoughton, 1939), p. 256.

14. Oliver O'Donovan, <u>The Problem of Self-Love in St. Augustine</u> (New Haven: Yale University Press, 1980), p. 37.

15. John C. Moore, <u>Love in Twelfth-Century France</u> (Philadelphia: University of Pennsylvania Press, 1972), p. 3.

16. William of St. Thierry, <u>The Nature and Destiny of Love</u>, trans. T. Davis (Kalamazoo, Michigan: Cistercian Publications, 1981), p.47.

17. Aelred of Rivaulx, <u>The Mirror of Charity</u>, trans. G. Webb and A. Walker (London: A.R. Maubray, 1962), p. 5.

18. Paul L. Williams, <u>The Moral Philosophy of Petere Abelard</u> (Lanham, Maryland: University Press of America, 1980), p. 79.

19. Etiénne Gilson, <u>Heloise and Abelard</u> (Ann Arbor, Michigan: University of Michigan Press, 1960), p. 56.

20. See Gilson, <u>La theologie mystique de saint Bernard</u> (Paris: J. Vrin, 1934), pp. 20-24.

21. Allen B. Wolter, "Duns Scotus," in Encyclopedia of Philosophy (New York: Macmillan, 1967), 2:434.

22. John Burnaby, op. cit., p. 275.

23. Meister Eckhart, "About Disinterest," trans. Raymond B. Blakney in Meister Eckhart (New York: Harper & Row, 1941), p. 88.

24. Ibid.

25. Martin Luther, Lectures on Romans, ed. Wilhelm Pauck (Philadelphia: Westminster Press, 1961), p. 163.

26. Karl Holl, The Reconstruction of Morality (Minneapolis: Augsburg, 1979), p. 36.

27. Wilhelm Pauck in his "Introduction" to Lectures on Romans. Op. cit., p. lv.

28. George W. Forrell, Faith Active in Love (Minneapolis: Augsburg, 1954), p. 95.

29. James Luther Adams made this comment on Nygren's Agape and Eros at a seminar at the University of Chicago Divinity School in 1980.

30. Roland H. Bainton, The Reformation in the Sixteenth Century (Boston: Beacon Press, 1952), p. 117.

31. Ibid.

32. Calvin, The Institutes of the Christian Religion, trans. F. Battles, ed. John T. McNeill (Philadelphia: The Westminster Press, 1960), III, 7, 1 on p. 690.

33. Barth as cited by John H. Leith, Introduction to

the Reformed Tradition (Atlanta: John Knox Press, 1978), p. 69.

34. Evelyn Underhill, The Mystics of the Church (New York: Schocken Books, 1964), pp. 210-211.

35. Fénelon's Dissertation on Pure Love was written in 1696, and published in 1750 in Germantown as Quakerism entered its so-called Quietist Period.

36. Austin Warren, New England Saints (Ann Arbor: University of Michigan Press, 1956), p. 64.

37. Ibid., p. 58.

38. John Dykstra Eusden's "Introduction" to William Ames, The Marrow of Theology, trans. J.D. Eusden (Durham, North Carolina: The Labyrinth Press, 1968), p. 1.

39. Ibid., p. 2.

40. William Ames, The Marrow of Theology, p. 250.

41. Ibid.

42. Ibid.

43. Ibid., p. 251.

44. Ibid., p. 252.

45. Ibid.

46. Eusden's "Introduction", p. 12.

47. Ibid., p. 15.

48. Ames, <u>The Marrow of Theology</u>, p. 303.

Chapter II

Self-Denial and Self-Love:
Early New England Theology

Thus far, I have highlighted a tension within the wider historical tradition of Christian thought regarding love and self-denial. While Augustine, Aquinas, and other figures who take the inclinations of human nature into account have no difficulty accommodating love for God with true self-love, this teleological ethic left some dissatisfied. Thus Abelard, Fénelon, and others rejected the Augustinian or eudaemonistic vision for a more absolute renunciation of all the preferences of the self. In the late seventeenth century, a parallel division is found in American theology. It eventually led to a fundamental debate within eighteenth-century Protestant thought. Therefore, to understand the eighteenth-century of Edwards and Hopkins, the agenda for the next chapters, some background discussion of earlier New England thought is essential.

Samuel Willard (d. 1707) was born in Concord, Massachusetts, in 1640. He graduated from Harvard in 1659, and went on to teach the orthodox theology of Puritanism there until called to the Old South Church in Boston. For a brief period beginning in 1700, Willard was acting president of Harvard while retaining his ministerial post.

Puritan theology of the time was grounded in the teachings of the <u>Westminster Catechism</u>, developed by the Westminster Assembly (1643-1649) which was formed in England for the purpose of reforming the Anglican Church along Calvinist Presbyterian lines. In 1687 Willard initiated a lecture series on the <u>Catechism</u> which continued monthly for twenty years until 1707. His lectures were published posthumously in 1726 under the title <u>A Complete Body of Divinity</u>.

In the introduction to his treatise, Willard writes that, "The substance of this inquiry may be reduced to two heads, or gathered up in two questions, viz., What is happiness, and how may it be obtained."[1] A more Augustinian statement would be difficult to find. Its presence at the outset of the treatise indicates that the theme of true happiness was sufficiently controversial to serve as the cornerstone of a popular series of talks. The place of true self-love or happiness in Christian ethics was, then, a topical question at the time — a time when the pure-love controversy seems to have engulfed most of Europe. As one historian puts it, Willard's lectures drew vast numbers of people from "all around the Boston area."[2]

Why Willard's reaffirmation of the Augustinian position? Willard viewed his task in part as one of response to the "willingness to be damned" theology which advocated radical self-denial. He rejected this ideal of selflessness in no uncertain

22

terms:

> Here, therefore, that great case with which some perplex themselves and others, is easily resolved, viz. Q. Whether a man ought willingly to be damned so God's glory may be advanced by it? Answ. A willingness to be damned is inconsistent with a true desire that God may be glorified: because it separates those things which God has made inseparable, it supposes a clashing in that very order, which God has put between the End and the means; . . . [3]

This passage stresses the "very order" of God's glorious creation, in which the "end" of salvation and the "means" of human nature correlate. The natural inclination towards happiness and the duty to glorify God are "things which God has made inseparable." Willard concludes his discussion as follows: "God having put into man a natural desire after happiness or well-being, makes use of it to help him in his duty."[4] Willard, then, is clearly a Puritan Augustinian for whom the concept of true "well-being" is central. He has no compromise to make with those extremists who would displace all forms of self-love with radical self-denial.

Willard's Augustinianism is rooted in a theology of creation and nature. He reprimands theologians who ignore nature, denying that "man is a creature that was made capable of happiness" and that this capacity is God's handiwork.[5] Radical self-denial and disinterest in one's own well-being violate the order of nature in which the human existence is grounded and embedded. Willard's entire treatise is anchored in the notion that the human yearns for the good that it might bring true happiness to the lover.

Willard was not convinced solely by this theology of creation in these matters, for scripture indicated to him the truth of Augustinianism as well. Radically disinterested love for God violates the Bibical passages that bring together "command and promise," i.e., which appeal to the yearnings of nature that God's will might be fulfilled: "God doth, as it were, say to the children of men, you have a desire to be happy; that you can only be in the enjoyment of me . . . . "[6] Scripture, then, convinces that God does not intend to abolish the structures of human desire in order to achieve salvation for persons; rather, God wants only to redirect the desires and affections, reordering them towards himself that happiness might be realized. Edwards, it will later be shown, was a Puritan Augustinian who, like Willard, recognized the correlation between nature and scripture.

God, Willard concludes, can only relate to persons in a fashion consistent with his created order. "In his wisdom," wrote Willard, "God deals with man in a way that is suited to his nature."[7] From the beginning of human existence, God's hope has been that persons would acknowledge "God alone as an adequate object for felicity."[8]

At least in part, the ethic of radical self-denial which Willard confronted has scriptural origins. Thus, he was impelled to comment on Romans 9:3, which apparently was used as a proof text for this ethic in the colonies as it had been earlier by the medieval mystics. This passage reads thus: "For I could even pray to be outcast from Christ myself for the sake of my brothers, my natural kinsfolk." For some, the passage implies the requirement that a Christian surrender participation in the mutual good in order to be truly loving. Willard refutes this reading, arguing that the passage presents only "a potential mood."[9] To interpret it as more than this is to "dishonor" a God who does not break promises.

The most systematic study of Willard's thought is that of Ernest Benson Lowrie, who analyzes A Complete Body of Divinity in detail. The following quotation from Lowrie's study reveals the

Augustinian themes in which we are interested:

> The entire theological edifice Willard constructs is anchored in the natural yearnings of the human spirit for an infinite good that will satisfy "all the reachings of the human soul" and gratify "all its appetites." By nature man is so insatiably desirous of happiness "that absolutely nothing can sever his deeper passions from this congenerate principle of human nature," . . . Man is a free moral agent who must bid for fulfillment.[10]

In sum, Lowrie concludes that Willard accomodated his theological ethic to the ontological constitution of human nature.

Willard was not alone in his affirmations of true self-love. He was indebted to another Puritan thinker, Thomas Watson (d. 1690). Watson's A Body of Divinity was published in 1692 and became popular on both sides of the Atlantic. Educated at Emmanuel College, Cambridge, Watson was eminent among the early British Puritans, and the author of numerous theological treatises. Watson never left England, but his impact on colonial Puritans was tremendous. Above all, he was a Puritan Augustinian.

One of the basic themes of Watson's treatise A Body of Divinity is the affirmation of proper self-love. God is both glorified and enjoyed simulanteously, for "God has twisted together his glory and our good."[11] Indeed, Watson writes, "the more happiness you have," the more "God will be glorified." There is a distinctly and uninhibited emphasis on the true joys that love for God brings to the lover, for God is "the sweet," the "juicy and spiced," and the "relished." This ecstatic sense of the delights God gives is captured here by langauge which Edwards would make use of in describing his conversion experiences several decades later.

That Watson was familiar with Augustine's works is clear, for at several junctures he cites the latter and adopts his basic eudaemonistic framework. Thus, the following passage informed by Augustine's The City of God:

> Let it be the chief end of our living to enjoy this chief good hereafter. Augustine reckons up to 288 opinions among the philosophers about happiness, but all were short of the mark. The highest elevation of a reasonable soul is to enjoy God forever.[12]

Watson, then, made extensive use of Augustine to the extent that the tendency to devalue all concern for personal well-being has no place in his ethics.

True felicity was, for Watson, the goal of religious life. Just as the body cannot have life without union with the soul, the soul without God is incapable of completion.

> As the body cannot have life but by having communion with the soul, so the soul cannot have blessedness but by having immediate communion with God. God is the Summum Bonum, the chief good; therefore the enjoyment of his is the highest felicity.[13]

This analog between the relation of body and soul to soul and God is explicitly Augustinian.

Another important Puritan contemporary of Willard who spent sixteen years in New England and then returned to London in 1648 was Giles Firmin (d. 1697). A medical doctor, Firmin came to New England in 1632, and was ordained a deacon under John Cotton. Having left his wife and children back in America, Firmin was called to a parish in England and never returned to the colonies. In 1670 he published his The Real Christian. The main theme of this treatise is that God would not require a love contrary to the desire for happiness. "In all God's Bible," writes Firmin, "there is not one duty that God requires of his creatures, which is contary to his creature's happiness . . . contrary to man as man . . .

determined by a natural inclination to its ultimate end, that is, blessedness."[14] Firmin was especially concerned to refute those who misrepresented Christian conversion experience such that all natural inclinations of the soul were forfeit. In conversion, he insisted, "not the least violence is offered anyone" with regard to "the workings of all the faculties of the soul, ..."[15] The notion of "the willingness to be damned" as a test of Christian virtue was particularly appalling to Firmin. As has been pointed out recently by one scholar, the controversy which Hopkins stirred due to his insistence on the extremes of self-denial really broke out "at the end of the eighteenth century" in both England and America such that Firmin devoted much attention to it.[16]

Without detailing the thought of Watson, Willard, and Firmin, it can be understood from the foregoing that the Puritan theologians were inspired by Augustinianism. Moreover, their involvement in a pure-love controversy within Puritanism was extensive enough for them to direct their major writings in the direction of an Augustinian solution. With some qualification, Edwards' theology lies firmly within the boundaries of Puritan Augustinian thought. Christian love is understood within this rich tradition as coextensive with proper self-love. Perhaps Willard summarized this strain best for the American Puritans when he claimed that God works with, rather than against, nature. Alas, there were those who maintained that all self-love must be abolished, rather than redirected towards the divine. Attention must now be given their ideas.

Disinterested Love in New England

For some, to love and glorify God entails a

thoroughly self-denying renunciation of self. Self-love and love in its Christian sense are thought to be utterly antithetical. Such dissatisfaction with the Augustinian strain among the Puritans is, in fact, quite pronounced.

It is more difficult to trace the origins of the pure love position in New England than it is the Augustinian. New Englanders were not reading French Catholic treatises on pure love, although Fénelon's major literary and metaphysical writings were available at Yale during the early decades of the eighteenth century. Though Fénelon's Dissertation on Pure Love was published in Pennsylvania in 1750 and achieved tremendous popularity, New Englanders were hardly interested in the "heretical" Quakers who made more of the Inner Light than of Holy Scripture. All that can be said is that the widespread debate over pure love in Europe was the common property of the colonies. Thus, in mid-nineteenth-century retrospect Samuel Hopkins' biographer, Edwards A. Park, noted a resemblance of the former to specific European mystics: "There is a striking resemblance between the feelings of Doctor Hopkins and the feelings of Fénelon, Madame Guyon, and many other mystics with regard to the endurance of pain for the divine glory."[17]

Sarah Peirpont Edwards was one swept up in the piety of pure love. Mrs. Edwards went through a period of intense spiritual experience which she recorded in her journals. The importance of her mystical experiences have been overlooked by many writers of American religious history, though William James gives them considerable attention in his The Varieties of Religious Experience. Mrs. Edwards writes that she found "her own will entirely subdued to his will"; moreover, she discovered within herself "a willingness to live and die in spiritual darkness, if the honor of God required it . . . ."[18] In another passage, she adds,

28

"Whether I was willing to be kept out of heaven even longer; and my whole heart seemed immediately to reply, 'yes, a thousand years, if it be God's will and for his honor and glory.'"[19] These passages rival the accounts of the most intense mystics with regard to the theme of self-denial. They also indicate that Mrs. Edwards took seriously that influential passage from St. Paul, Romans 9:3, which Willard had struggled to remove from the hands of pure-love advocates.

It must immediately be added that Mrs. Edwards was the "spiritual mother" of Samuel Hopkins, i.e., she was the primary influence on his conversion experience. During this youthful period of quest, Hopkins spent many days at the Edwards' home under Mrs. Edwards' spiritual guidance. In addition to his "consistent Calvinism," Mrs. Edwards' influence must also be taken into account when discussing his doctrine of Christian love in which the last iota of self-love is driven from the heart.[20] Of course Hopkins' ethic of self-denial has been rightly attributed to his reaction against the greed and selfishness of Yankee economic acquisitiveness, especially as he witnessed it in the context of the Newport slave trade.[21] Joseph Conforti has written that Hopkins' rejection of all self-love was informed by his "experience of the worldly society and commercial economy of Newport."[22] But in the final analysis, it is necessary to take into serious consideration Hopkins' spiritual biography and the place Mrs. Edwards played in it.

That the precedents to Mrs. Edwards are difficult to specify is not to suggest that views close to her own were not articulated. There were some who went far in the direction of making radical self-denial an end in itself. In the 1630's Thomas Hooker stressed a form of "contrition" as the first stage of conversion requiring that the heart be "broken to pieces," a view against which Firmin and Willard specifically reacted. As Hooker put it,

"A contrite heart is that which is powdered all to dust, . . . "[23] Finally, the believer is left with no assurance of salvation, for he or she "cannot tell whether my father will receive me or no."[24] But even here, the severity of self-denial is mitigated by the knowledge that because one is willing to renounce all well-being, salvation is likely in store. Thus Hooker writes of the "secret hope of mercy, wherewith God supports the hearts of those who are truly broken . . . ."[25] So while Hooker (as well as Thomas Shepard) prescribed radical indifference to one's well-being, the unspoken likelihood of salvation permits hope. Multitudes of New England preachers, argues G. N. Boardman, "taught entire submission to the government of God," but such submission carried with it the glimmer of hope.[26]

Somehow, a transition occurred in which even the glimmer of hope was lost. In an earlier chapter, the guarded suggestion was made that perhaps Cotton Mather is of particular importance with regard to the developing ethic of radical self-denial in American circles. He did remark that "the Quietists are the best Christians," and his appropriation of Lutheran Pietist impulses is considerable.[27] It may be that with Mather, a more total rejection of self-love entered upon the American scene, though this is only a suggested avenue. If cast off forever by a righteous God, Mather counsels the Christian to "forever silence all murmuring against him."[28]

Certainly we know that Mather, in a number of his better known sermons, devoted his efforts to a critique of Puritan Augustinian language. In a sermon preached on September 8, 1713, in Boston, Mather begins with a citation from the Gospel of John: "The cup which my Father has given me, shall I not drink it?"[29] The theology of the Cross, not of nature, provides the framework for this fearful message. It is Jesus who serves as the model of Christian fulfillment, for he was "full of resignation to the will of his Father, in all the sufferings appointed him!"[30] The endurance of suffering is the primary Christian virtue here, rather than love. As Christ suffered, so must the Christian. There is absolutely no reference to the limits on self-denial imposed upon persons by nature and social existence. All Christians are called on to follow the path of crucifixion, such that radical self-denial becomes normative. "For me to resemble my admirable savior," writes Mather, "particularly in taking patiently, whatever cup shall, be by my Heavenly Father given me, this always is my duty; this always will be my glory!"[31] The resonance here with the Quietists such as Fénelon, whom Mather admired, is striking. In all of this, Mather was running against the grain of orthodox Puritan Augustinian ideas with their general appreciation of true self-love.

With regard to the Augustinian language, Mather had little patience. "You cannot expect," he wrote, "always to hear no other invitation but this, 'Drink the sweet!'"[32] For, he continues, the "desire for happiness" must "vanish before the will of God."[33] All of this effort to expunge Puritanism of the Augustinian taint once and for all may have set the spirituality of Mrs. Edwards and Hopkins in motion.

Whatever the source, a radical critique of Augustinianism won its place in the American theological tradition. During the eighteenth century, the ideal of a completely disinterested love for God and neighbor emerged as a viable alternative. It may be that the Augustinian position became corrupted by a worldliness such that the material prosperity it was said God guarantees, i.e., "external" rewards, replaced God himself as the object of desire. Augustinianism played into the hands of ministers who were quite willing to overlook its proscriptions against selfishness in order to sell Christianity to a generation distanced from the faith of its Fathers. Thus, for instance, the writings of John Webb, who in his 1721 Boston lectures argued that young people should turn to the God who brings "food and raiment and other necessaries and conveniences of life" such as "a good name, credit, and reputation."[34] The Christianity of Yankee mercantilism was on the rise, and ministers such as Webb and Jonathan Mayhew altered Augustinianism to accommodate an increasingly acquisative society. As Augustinianism degenerated into an ideology for economic gain, disinterested love perhaps arose as a critical alternative. Eventually, the Hopkinsians would claim that even the highest forms of self-love are still self-love, soon to be transformed into "devouring beasts." Thus Hopkins engaged in various pamphlet wars against Mayhew in which he expressed his dissatisfaction with Christian appeals to self-love.

The debate between American theologians regarding the degree to which Christian love requires self-denial raged on among the Edwardseans and other into the next century. Two decades after Hopkins' death, William Channing, a boyhood member of Hopkins' Newport congregation, would condense the latter's ethic to a single phrase, "the entire surrender of personal interest."[35] Clearly Hopkins bequethed a legacy different from that of Edwards.

One qualification with regard to Edwards is in order here. While Edwards was fundamentally writing within the Augustinian framework, he did have some appreciation for the ideal of radically self-denying love as well. To an extent, he tried to encompass this ideal within his ethic, thus articulating the tradition of Puritan Augustinianism in a modified form. It is from this tension that a complex and even unique American theological ethic was born. Impressed by the notion of disinterested love Edwards made very carefully circumscribed use of it. Yet Edwards does not represent a third type, lying somewhere betwixt and between Augustinianism and pure love. Rather, he was fundamentally Augustinian in his views.

Footnotes

1. Samuel Willard, <u>A Complete Body of Divinity in Two Hundred and Fifty Expository Lectures on the Assembly's Shorter Catechism</u> (Boston: B. Green and S. Kneeland, 1726), p. 1.

2. James W. Jones, <u>The Shattered Synthesis: New England Puritanism Before the Great Awakening</u> (New Haven and London: Yale University Press, 1973), p. 55.

3. Willard, <u>op. cit.,</u> p. 4.

4. <u>Ibid.</u>

5. <u>Ibid.,</u> p. 2.

6. <u>Ibid.,</u> p. 4.

7. <u>Ibid.,</u> p. 11.

8. <u>Ibid.,</u> p. 7.

9. <u>Ibid.,</u> p. 5.

10. Ernest Benson Lowrie, <u>The Shape of the Puritan Mind: The Thought of Samuel Willard</u> (New Haven and London: Yale University Press, 1974), p. 24.

11. Thomas A. Watson, <u>A Body of Divinity</u> (London: Banner of Truth Press, 1971), p. 13.

12. <u>Ibid.,</u> p. 24.

13. <u>Ibid.,</u> p. 23.

14. Giles Firmin, <u>The Real Christian</u> (Evans Microfilm Copy of 1670 edition), p. 141.

15. <u>Ibid.</u>, p. 29.

16. James W. Jones, <u>op. cit.</u>, p. 37.

17. Edwards A. Park, "Memoir," in <u>The Works of Samuel Hopkins</u> (Boston: Doctrinal Book and Tract Society, 1954), 1:211.

18. Sereno E. Dwight cites these passages from Mrs. Edwards's "Journal" in his "Memoirs of Jonathan Edwards," <u>The Works of Jonathan Edwards</u> (London: Banner of Truth Press, 1979 edition), 1: p. ixix.

19. <u>Ibid.</u>, 1: p. ixvii.

20. Frank Hugh Foster provides a useful discussion of "consistent Calvinism" in <u>A Genetic History of New England Theology</u> (Chicago: University of Chicago Press, 1907), Chapter 6.

21. See Richard L. Bushman on Yankee economic life in <u>From Puritan to Yankee</u> (New York: W.W. Norton, 1967), p. 278.

22. Joseph A. Conforti, <u>Samuel Hopkins and the New Divinity Movement</u> (Grand Rapids, Michigan: William D. Eerdmans, 1981), p. 125.

23. Thomas Hooker, <u>The Unbeliever's Preparing for Christ</u>, in <u>Works of Rev. Thomas Hooker</u>, compiled by George B. Ide (London, 1638), 1:147.

24. <u>Ibid.</u>, 1:195.

25. <u>Ibid.</u>, 1:192.

26. G. N. Boardman, <u>A History of New England</u>

<u>Theology</u> (New York: A. D. F. Randolph Co., 1899), p.147.

27. Richard F. Lovelace, <u>The American Pietism of Cotton Mather</u> (Grand Rapids, Michigan: William B. Eerdmans, 1979), p. 159.

28. <u>Ibid.</u>

29. Cotton Mather, <u>The Will of A Father Submitted To</u> (Boston: Thomas Fleet, 1713), p. 3.

30. <u>Ibid.</u>, p. 18.

31. <u>Ibid.</u>, p. 26.

32. <u>Ibid.</u>

33. <u>Ibid.</u>, p. 27.

34. John Webb, <u>The Peculiar Advantages of Early Piety</u> (Boston: S. Kneeland, 1721), p. 80.

35. William Channing, as cited by Edwards A. Park in "Memoir," <u>op. cit.</u>, 1:210.

Chapter III

Edwards' Theology of Love

It was shown in the previous chapter that the traditional tension between Augustinianism and disinterested (or pure and indifferent) love converged on seventeenth-century Christianity in New England. This tension is an hermeneutical key into the New England mind that has been largely neglected. In the exposition of the thought of Edwards which follows, I will focus on this tension in order to clarify his theology of love.

Conrad Cherry contrasts Edwards, the theologian of love, with Luther, the theologian of faith, and concludes that, "Love to God finds an emphasis in Edwards' Protestant thought unparalleled by the earliest Protestant reformers."[1] Though Cherry does not discuss the seventeenth-century tension regarding the concepts of love, he does comment that Edwards " . . . stands in much more affinity with his own century than he does with the sixteenth."[2] In fact, Edwards was in part an eighteenth-century theologian responding to a set of seventeenth-century concerns over love for God and self-love which were still vital during his period. Throughout his career, Edwards viewed love as the essence of religion, and in one of his last works wrote thus: "The very quintessence of all religion, the very thing wherein lies summarily the sincerity, spirituality, and divinity of religion. And that, the apostle teaches, is love."[3] Furthermore, Edwards was sufficiently indebted to the Augustinianism of Willard and Stoddard to avoid defining Christian love primarily in terms of disinterestedness.

The Augustinian Element

The total rejection of self-love, characteristic of the Hopkinsians, who popularized the notion of disinterested benevolence, has been erroneously attributed to Edwards. There are at least five reasons why Edwards was unwilling to strip Christian ethics of the Augustinian element: First, he appreciated the intellectual heritage of Firmin, Willard, and his maternal grandfather Solomon Stoddard all of whom were suspicious of the radical renunciation of the human inclination toward happiness; second, during the course of the Northampton revivals, Edwards was distressed by several suicides which he attributed to melancholy and the religiously inspired ideal of self-abnegation rooted in the Quietist notion of the resignatio ad infernum which had established itself in the minds of some New Englanders, including his wife; third, he defined the will as always seeking its own good and thus had empirical doubts about the notion of a selfless love; fourth, Edwards was convinced that Scripture promises rewards and happiness, and understood this to be the cornerstone of the prudential aspect of Christian ethics; and finally, he viewed God as the exemplar of happiness sharing this attribute with the saints through the Holy Spirit. Each of these reasons for retaining an Augustinian element requires clarification.

Early in his career, Edwards acknowledged the influence of Stoddard. The following passage taken from one of Stoddard's sermons indicates his Augustinian framework: "The first and great commandment is to love the Lord thy God with all thy heart, Matt. 22:37-38. There is much of a spirit of self-love in the saint; but other men are under the power of it."[4] The natural man, argued Stoddard, is not destroyed by Christianity. Natural self-love is not eradicated, but rather properly directed by grace. Edwards, in his Miscellany 301, affirmed that "Mr. Stoddard of this town of Northampton" developed the "best philosophy that I have met with of original sin" because "that natural and necessary inclination that man has to his own benefit" is not thrust aside.[5] Edwards clearly associated himself with Puritan orthodoxy insofar as it admitted true self-love into Christian ethics.

Yet it would be wrong to attribute Edwards' Augustinianism solely to traditional loyalties. Practical interests persuaded him that the emphasis on the rightful role of the desire for happiness in Christian fulfillment was an absolute necessity for his own well-being and that of his congregation. Gail Thain Parker, in her article "Jonathan Edwards and Melancholy," points out that between 1722 and 1724 Edwards made at least six resolutions in his diary which admit of personal melancholy, for in the 1720's "he recognized the workings of the disease in his own mind."[6] Parker notes that Edwards was also distressed by the "epidemic" of melancholy in the Northampton revivals of the 1730's as well as in the later Awakening, and then argues that Edwards' Treatise on the Religious

Affections can be interpreted as an effort to separate melancholy from "true religious affections." Edwards did associate melancholy with the work of Satan in the Religious Affections, adding substance to Parker's claim.[7]

In 1736, Edwards wrote his A Faithful Narrative of Surprising Conversions, a reflection on the Northampton revival. There had been at least one suicide during the revival, and Edwards' reaction to the event is expressed in a wider critique of extreme humiliation:

> Some, when in such circumstances, have felt that sense of the excellency of God's justice, appearing in the vindictive exercises of it, against such sinfulness as theirs was; and have now such a submission of mind in their idea of this attribute, and of the exercises of it — together with an exceeding loathing of their own unworthiness, and a kind of indignation against themselves — that they have sometimes called it a willingness to be damned; though it must be owned that they had not a clear and distinct idea of damnation, nor does any word in the Bible require such self-denial as this.[8]

This anti-Quietist position is supported by the conviction that empirically speaking, no person can will to be unhappy. Though, as Edwards put it, ". . . they see the glory of God would shine bright in their own condemnation; and they are ready to think that if they are damned, they could take part with God against themselves, and would glorify his justice therein . . . " such extreme self-abnegation contradicts human nature.[9] Norman Fiering, in a study of Edwards' moral thought, takes note of Edwards' anti-Quietism.[10] Edwards was convinced that because human nature necessarily pursues its own good, the test of "willingness to be damned" is incoherent; moreover, it disguises a pathological melancholy leading to self-destruction with an air

of sanctity. That Edwards was so adament on this
point again demonstrates that the Quietist emphasis
on the resignatio ad infernum, perhaps directly or
through its impact on the German Pietists with
whom Mather corresponded, had emerged as a
significant element in New England piety during
the 1730's.[11]

Edwards developed his polemic against
melancholy and the resignatio ad infernum in a
collection of sermons written in 1738 entitled
Charity and Its Fruits and published posthumously.
While he affirmed the virtue of humility, that is, "a
sense of our meanness as compared with God, or a
sense of the infinite distance there is between God
and ourselves," not all humility is "true" humility.
As he put it, some have "a low thought of
themselves" from a "melancholy and desponding
temperament which is natural to them . . . ."[12]
Melancholics might think themselves to be
humble, when in fact "they have no true humility." _humble_
Moreover, Edwards argued that truly virtuous
humility does not include a tendency toward radical
self-denial, for "If Christianity did indeed tend to
destroy man's love for himself, and to his own
happiness, it would threaten to destroy the very
spirit of humanity . . . ."[13] That the saint seeks true
happiness "is as necessary to his own nature as the
faculty of the will is; and it is impossible that such a
love should be destroyed in any other way than by
destroying his being."[14] Contrary to the doctrine of
resignatio ad infernum, Edwards was certain that
the more the saint loved God, the "more happiness
is pursued."

It is in the light of his polemic against
melancholy masquerading as Christian virtue that
Edwards' emphasis on hope can be properly
appreciated — an emphasis, incidentally, found in
the thought of Fénelon's critics in France. In
Charity and Its Fruits Edwards articulated a theology
of hope which is based on Scripture and experience.

Edwards was convinced with Paul that the theological virtues of hope and love are inseparable. Edwards introduced his discussion of hope with a citation from I Corinthians 13:7, "Charity . . . believeth all things, hopeth all things."[15] From this Edwards concluded that among the fruits of charity is the "tendency to promote the graces of faith and hope, which are such great graces of the gospel."[16] Paul, Edwards stressed, mentioned the "three graces of faith, hope, and charity, together." Thus, there is a fundamental unity between the theological virtues which Edwards likened to the links of a chain:

> That the graces of Christianity are all connected together, and mutually dependent on each other. That is, they are all linked together, and united one to another and within another, as links of a chain are; and one does, as it were, hang on another, from one end of the chain to the other, so that, if one link be broken, all fall to the ground, and th whole ceases to be of any effect.[17]

This is, then, "the manner in which the graces of Christianity are connected."

In developing the connection between the theological virtues of love and hope, Edwards used the analogy of the relationship between child and father: "And so love tends to hope, for the spirit of love is the spirit of a child, and the more any one feels himself this spirit toward God, the more natural it will be to him to look to God, to go to God as his father.[18] He also maintained that the theological virtues of faith, hope, and love are all from the same source:

> The graces of Christianity are all from the same Spirit of Christ sent forth into the heart, and dwelling there as a holy and powerful, and divine nature; as there may be different reflections of the light of the sun, and yet all in origin the same kind of light,

because it all comes from the same source or body of light.[19]

These and other arguments based on Edwards' observations accord with Scripture and unmask melancholy posing as virtue. In later writings, Edwards continued to develop his theology of hope though he always remained consistent with these early reflections in <u>Charity and Its Fruits</u>.[20] Despite his harsh sermons on the damnation of sinners in the hands of an angry God, Edwards carefully guarded against the abolition of hope.

Edwards, then, was committed to the Augustinian theme in the theology of his New England forebears; moreover, he articulated a theology of hope in response to melancholy and the <u>resignatio ad infernum</u>. However, the influence of John Locke, whose <u>An Essay Concerning Human Understanding</u> made a lasting impression of Edwards from his youth, was also a factor in his retention of Augustinianism.

It would be difficult to imagine Edwards rejecting the notion that human nature's pursuit of happiness must be accommodated in any image of Christian fulfillment given Locke's position. Locke wrote extensively on happiness, particularly in the section of his <u>An Essay</u> entitled "On Power." Here Locke developed his theory of desire, which he defined as "being nothing but an uneasiness in the want of an absent good . . ."[21] And what is it that "moves desire?" Locke responded, " . . . happiness, and that alone."[22] Happiness, he added, "is the utmost pleasure we are capable of . . . "[23] Locke did not think that the desire for happiness could be suspended, referring to it as an "unalterable pursuit."[24] In <u>The Nature of True Virtue</u>, written by Edwards near the end of his life, his acknowledgement of the "unalterable" dimension of the pursuit of happiness is clear in passages such as this: "so that every being who has a faculty of will, must of necessity have an inclination to happiness."[25] To pursue one's own misery, argued by some to be the mark of true humility, was to Edwards a psychological impossibility.

There is a theological context in which Locke expressed his thoughts on pursuit of happiness. Locke insisted that God is a being of perfect happiness, and that the happy person is God's image: "God Almighty himself is under the necessity of being happy; and the more any intelligent being is so, the nearer is its approach to infinite perfection and happiness."[26] Edwards likewise stressed the supreme happiness of God, and argued elaborately regarding God's communication of his happiness to the saint. When Divine perfection becomes the model of human perfection, and an aspect of Divine perfection is infinite happiness, selfless love becomes an inappropriate ideal.

Edwards sought truth in Scripture as well as in experience; he was convinced that though revealed truth goes beyond empirical truth, the former never contradicts the latter. Thus, in addition to his Lockean convictions regarding the pursuit of happiness, Edwards found warrants in Scripture for the Augustinian recognition of the role of self-love in the Christian ethic. In Charity and Its Fruits he wrote that "from one end of the Bible to the other" there are appeals to "the principle of self-love." Scripture, in frankly prudential fashion, "counsels to seek our own good" and warns to "beware of misery."[27] To undermine this element of the Biblical ethic would be, argued Edwards, to open the door to "melancholy and desponding temperament."[28] Given the influence of Reformed covenant theologians on Edwards, it comes as no surprise that the promissory note in Scripture was central in Edwards' refutation of the Quietist theme of resignatio ad infernum.[29]

That happiness is a Christian virtue is also substantiated, held Edwards, by the very character of

God. Sanctification in Edwards' thought can be defined broadly as the saintly manifestation of the love and happiness which characterizes God's perfection. The degree to which Edwards emphasized the happiness of God is striking. In his <u>An Essay on the Trinity</u>, written late in his career and published posthumously, the generation of infinite happiness in the Godhead is explained:

> Tis common when speaking of the divine happiness to say that God is infinitely happy in the enjoyment of Himself, in perfections, and accordingly it must be supposed that God perpetually and eternally has a most perfect idea of Himself, ever before Him and in actual view, and from hence arises a most pure and perfect act or energy in the Godhead, which is the Divine love, complacence and joy.[30]

God's "idea of Himself" is the projection of his own perfection, and is "absolutely perfect and therefore is an express and perfect image of Him, exactly like Him in every respect."[31] Edwards' thought accords with the idealism of George Berkeley here: "This representation of the Divine nature and essence is the Divine nature and essence again: so that by God's <u>thinking</u> of the deity must certainly be generated. Hereby there is another person begotten . . ."[32] And Edwards identified this generated essence with "the dearly beloved Son of God." Christ, then is viewed as begotten by the Father through the process of projection.

God's happiness results from the Father's joy in relationship with his Son, for "God undoubtedly infinitely loves and delights in the understanding and view of His own glorious essence: this is commonly said. The same scripture teaches us concerning the image of God that is His Son."[33] As Edwards again put it, "The infinite happiness of the Father consists in the enjoyment of His Son: Prov. viii, 30, I was daily His delight, i.e., before the world was."[34] The happiness the Father experiences in viewing his own essence was likened by Edwards to a man who "sees his own face in a looking glass."[35] The Son, too, experiences infinite happiness in the Godhead because he in turn delights in the Father's perfection. As Edwards maintained, both "God and the idea of God" are perfectly happy.

From this mutual love between Father and Son proceeds the Holy Spirit: "There proceeds a most pure act, and an infinitely holy and sacred energy between the Father and the Son in mutually loving and delighting in each other, for their love is mutual."[36] This sacred energy is identified by Edwards with the Holy Spirit, the vehicle through which God communicates love and happiness to man. Happiness is poured into the saints by the Spirit as "light from the sun" or "sap from a tree."[37] This communication of happiness to the creature does not, held Edwards, mean that God's happiness depends on the happiness of the creature; God is already perfectly happy and "overflows" with it as the sun emits its light.[38]

Edwards, then, viewed God as sharing the infinite plentitude of his happiness with the saints. This metaphysical position agrees with his conviction that Scripture is good news, as well as with his use of passages such as the following: (Matthew 8:2) "If ye then, being evil, know how to give good gifts to your children, how much more shall your Father in heaven, give good things to them that ask Him!"[39] It is important to bear in mind that Edwards, during his youthful conversion experiences, was struck by his immediate sense of peace and happiness. He was convinced that true conversion brings with it perfect joy.

Much more could be said regarding Edwards' appreciation of the Augustinian element of New England Puritan thought, his concern with melancholy, his Lockean and empiricist position on the pursuit of happiness, his use of Scripture, and

46

his concept of an overflow of Divine happiness. I have dealt with these themes in Edwards' thought to show that while disinterested love played a role in Edwards' thought, he was unwilling to turn away from Augustinianism. Yet while Edwards never discarded the Augustinian tradition, he added the element of disinterested love to it. The ideal of a disinterested love, a love that "seeketh not its own," appealed to him as well.

The Role of Disinterested Love

Though Edwards underscored the proper place of true self-love in <u>Charity and Its Fruits</u>, he somewhat paradoxically introduced the concept of disinterested benevolence in the same text. Edwards apparently viewed Augustinianism and disinterested love as compatible. The following passage indicates the "free and disinterested" element in Edwards' theology of love:

> And therefore there is no other love so much above the selfish principle as Christian love is; no love that is so free and disinterested, and in the exercise of which God is so loved for Himself and His own sake, and men are loved, not because of their relation to self, but because of their relation to God as His children . . . [40]

God is to be loved not because such love brings happiness; rather, God is loved strictly for his own sake. As Edwards put it, "Though all real love to others seeks the good and espouses the interests of those who are beloved, yet all other love, excepting this, has its foundation, in one sense, in the selfish principle."[41] The peculiar" nature of this disinterested love for both God and the neighbor is "that it is above the selfish principle." Mere natural love, by contrast, cannot "go beyond self-love . . . "[42]

47

Despite all his arguments to the effect that Christianity does not "go against" human nature, Edwards here maintained that there is a higher religious affection which goes beyond nature's limits. Such affection is a gift of grace.

How did Edwards reconcile Augustinian and disinterested love in <u>Charity and Its Fruits</u>? To the extent that he was able to do so, he relied on a complex theological anthropology. He posited a structural dichotomy in the regenerate — a two-story image of saintly perfection. On the lower floor is the "natural principle," and the "offspring of natural principles" is self-love.[43] While the reprobates are limited to this lower floor, the regenerate are blessed with a "supernatural principle" of which disinterested or "divine love is the offspring."[44] On the higher floor is the supernatural principle from which disinterested love flows spontaneously "above and beyond all that is natural." Edwards likened the supernatural principle to " a plant transplanted into the soul out of the garden of heaven, by the holy and blessed Spirit of God, and so has life in God, and not in self."[45] The saint manifests an unconditional disinterested love which is, metaphysically speaking, none other than the divine love generated in the Godhead which pours itself out through the Holy Spirit. The importance of the "supernatural principle" — the second floor of Edwards' theological anthropology — should not obscure the continued significance of the natural principle, for otherwise Christianity would "destroy the very spirit of humanity." Grace completes natures, it does not destroy it. Thus, Edwards, in <u>Charity and Its Fruits</u>, responded positively to the ideal of disinterested love while remaining firmly anchored in Augustinianism. This position of delicate balance provided the framework for much of his later writing.

This framework is evident in one of his best

known works, <u>A Treatise Concerning Religious Affections</u>, written in 1746 in the aftermath of the First Great Awakening, during which Edwards continued to develop his theology of love. He retained the two-story theological anthropology articulated in <u>Charity and Its Fruits</u>, and elaborated on the relationship between natural and disinterested love. He was less concerned with melancholy and the refutation of the <u>resignatio ad infernum</u> than he was earlier. One important polemic in the <u>Religious Affections</u> is against those claiming that Christian love is nothing more than self-love focused on the hope for happiness. Edwards' task was to establish the disinterested element of religious affections. The following passage typifies his response to the argument that Christian love does not "go beyond the natural principle":

> The first objective ground of gracious affections is the transcendentally excellent and amiable nature of divine things, as they are in themselves; and not a <u>conceived</u> relation they bear to self, or self-interest.[46]

This passage defines the second sign of true religious affections, and indicates that Edwards sought to put even true and acceptable self-love in its place. The polemic nature of this sign is evident from the following:

> Some say that all love arises from self-love; and that it is impossible in the nature of things, for any man to have love to God, or any other being, but that love to himself must be the foundation of it.[47]

Edwards disputed those holding that "whoever loves God, and so desires his glory, or the enjoyment of him, he desires these things as his own happiness . . . "[48] It is the claim that God <u>can be loved only</u> "from self-love, or a desire of his own happiness" that disturbed Edwards.

With this polemic in mind, Edwards makes a

complicated statement:

> There is no doubt, but that <u>after</u> God's glory, and the beholding his perfections, are become so agreeable to him, that he places the highest happiness in these things, <u>then</u> he will desire them, as he desires his own happiness.[49] [my underlining]

In other words, prior to all consideration of self-interest or happiness, God is to be loved. True religious affection begins without any "preconceived relation to self" in mind, for "there is such a thing, as a kind of love or affection, . . . which does not properly arise from self-love . . . "[50] Of course Edwards acknowledged that true self-love "may be the foundation of great affections toward God and Christ," but this is not the "foundation" of the saint's love. As Edwards put it, "the true saint's superstructure is the hypocrite's foundation."[51] By this he meant that the true saint manifests a love for God which is grounded in disinterested affection, while the hypocrite's love for God is indeed completely reducible to self-love. Those who seize upon the affections of the hypocrite to discredit the Christian ethic as strictly prudential have ignored the loftier element of true religious affections.

Edwards' approach to the problem of balancing Augustinian and disinterested love has affinities with the British aesthetic philosophy of his day. Lord Shaftesbury and Francis Hutcheson attacked the theory of psychological egoism, i.e., the view that all affection can be attributed to self-love, by describing the so-called "aesthetic attitude." Monroe C. Beardsley touches on this in his comments on Shaftesbury:

> Just as he was led to face directly the question by what faculty beauty is apprehended, so Shaftesbury also took a close look at the phenomenology of that apprehension, and in so doing he helped to formulate a notion

that was to have a long and significant later history. He got into the problem of what is now called "aesthetic attitude" by reflecting on the theory of psychological egoism, which was so much in the air around the turn of the century. Are all human actions selfish?[52]

In response to the theory of psychological egoism, Shaftesbury turned toward a phenomenological description of the human encounter with beauty. As a counter to the views of Hobbes and Mandeville, and in striking resonance with Edwards, Shaftesbury wrote thus:

> And though the reflected joy or pleasure which arises from the notice of this pleasure once perceived, may be interpreted a self-passion or interested regard, yet the original satisfaction can be no other than what results from the love of truth, proportion, order and symmetry in the things without.[53]

In the initial moment of perception, then, self-love has no place. Francis Hutcheson, borrowing from Shaftesbury, held that the immediate perception of beauty has no relation to the prospect of personal advantage, though pleasure is "superadded" later in the aesthetic experience.[54]

Edwards as well maintained that only _after_ beholding God's perfection does the desire for true happiness enter into true religious affections; this is consistent with the aesthetic thought of his period. His argument was empirical, namely, that commonplace reflection on the experience of "loveliness or excellency" indicates that God, the most beautiful of all beings, is not always loved as a means to the end of personal happiness. As Arthur Cushman McGiffert writes regarding Edwards:

> At the first sight of beauty, one has no experience to go by. One does not know that beauty feeds the soul. One only knows that it is something altogether lovely and one

yields to it.[55]

Likewise, Norman Fiering alludes to the disinterested response to beauty.[56]

Drawing on a description of the aesthetic experience, Edwards concluded his discussion: "The saint's affections begin with God; and self-love has a hand in these affections consequently and secondarily only . . . "[57] Apparently Edwards was satisfied with this position, because in one of his last works, A Treatise on Grace, he developed an argument similar to that found in the Religious Affections as follows:

> But Divine love is a principle distinct from self-love, and from all that arise from it. Indeed, after a man is come to relish the sweetness of the supreme good there is in the nature of God, self-love may have a hand in an appetite after the enjoyment of that good. For self-love will necessarily make a man to desire to enjoy that which is sweet to men, or they must first have a taste to relish sweetness in the perfection of God, before self-love can have any influence upon them to cause an appetite after the enjoyment of that sweetness. And therefore that divine taste or relish of the soul, wherein Divine love doth most fundamentally consist, is prior to all influence that self-love can have to incline us to God; and so must be a principle quite distinct from it, and independent of it.[58]

"Divine love" here can be equated with disinterested love in that it is "quite distinct" from the natural principle, i.e., self-love.

Yet it is mistaken to think that Edwards relied exclusively on aesthetics in responding to the reduction of religious affections to self-love alone. In the Religious Affections, he found a strong warrant for disinterested love in Scripture, and particularly in Luke 6:32. As he put it, "Christ plainly speaks of this kind of love, as what is nothing beyond the love of wicked men, Luke 6:32: 'If ye love them that love you, what thank have ye? For sinners also love those that love them.'"[59] By "this kind of love" Edwards meant that love as much found in the "hearts of devils as angels" which stems from the natural principle, and held that it is this love of which Christ was critical.[60] Sinners can only love on the condition of reward, but saints love unconditionally. Edwards also found a warrant for disinterested love in the Book of Job. Edwards argued that Job loved God at the cost of his well-being. He specifically cited Job 1:9, "Doth Job serve God for nought!"[61]

In citing Luke 6:32, Edwards was indebted to Thomas Shepard, who made use of this passage in his Parable of the The Virgins, to which Edwards refers in the Religious Affections. In the context of his discussion of Luke 6:32, Edwards acknowledged a general appreciation of Shepard's distinction between "a natural love to Christ, as to one that does thee good . . . and spiritual . . ."[62]

However, in his discussion of the "second sign", Edwards also cited passages from Scripture such as I John 4:19 in support of the role of self-love in love for God, i.e., to show that "self-love is not excluded from a gracious attitude . . ."[63] He was willing to accommodate such passages so long as it is recognized that "another love prepares the way, and lays the foundation" for the participation of true self-love in religious affection. It can be inferred that Edwards' opponents had made use of these passages without such a recognition:

Some may perhaps be ready to object against the whole that has been said, that text, "We love him, because he first loved us" (I John 4:19), as though this implied that God's love to the true saints were the first foundation of their love to him.[64]

But Edwards interprets this passage as being

relevant to the "superstructure" of the saint's love for God, and not its foundation.

Edwards, then, was a Puritan Augustinian, yet one with real appreciation for the ideal of a pure disinterested love of "holy indifference." While a love beyond the limits of the "natural principle" does have a significant place in his ethic, it is carefully contained within the Augustinian framework.

The Nature of True Virtue

One of Edwards' last works, The Nature of True Virtue, can be interpreted in the light of the above analysis. The notion of pure or disinterested love enters this treatise as benevolent love "to being simply considered." It is not the love of gratitude, nor a love of attraction predicated on the virtue and beauty of the beloved.[65] It does not love because beings "love us" first. Nevertheless, for all this talk of benevolence, Edwards qualifies repeatedly with passages such as the following: "I say true virtue primarily consists in this. For I am far from asserting, that there is no virtue in any other love than this absolute benevolence."[66] For to limit Christian love to pure benevolence would be to contradict his many arguments embracing the natural principle of true self-love. The love of benevolence is "the primary objective foundation" of virtue, or in the terms of Religious Affections, it is the "foundation" as distinct from "super-structure."[67]

But the superstructure is still retained. Thus, love of gratitude and complacence figure in the nature of virtue. "Self-love," writes Edwards, "is far from being useless in the world, yea, it is exceedingly necessary to society; yet every body sees that if it not be subordinate to, and regulated by another more extensive principle, it may make a man a common enemy of the general system."[68] Here Edwards affirms the place of self-love in his ethical system. Sin is not true self-love, but selfishness: "All sin has its source from selfishness, or from self-love not subordinate to a regard to being in general."[69] Edwards has no interest in moving towards an ethic of radical self-denial, for "every being who has a faculty of will, must of necessity have an inclination to happiness."[70]

True Virtue, then, is Edwards' rearticulation of the parameters within which pure or benevolent love for God or neighbor must be placed. Unlike Hopkins, Edwards did not allow benevolence to throw all self-love to the winds. It is to Hopkins' notion of radically self-denying love that attention turns in the next chapter.

Footnotes

1. Conrad Cherry, <u>The Theology of Jonathan Edwards</u> (New York: Anchor Doubleday, 1966), p. 77.

2. <u>Ibid</u>, p. 78.

3. Jonathan Edwards, <u>Treatise in Grace</u> in <u>Treatise in Grace and Other Posthumously Published Writings</u>, edited, with an introduction by Paul Helm, (Cambridge: James Clarks and Co., Ltd., 1971), p. 44.

4. Solomon Stoddard, <u>That Natural Men are Under the Government of Self-Love</u> in his <u>Three Sermons</u> (Evans Microcard Edition, 1930), p. 36.

5. Edwards, "Miscellany 301," <u>The Philosophy of Jonathan Edwards</u>, ed. by Harvey G. Townsend (Eugene, Oregon: University of Oregon Press, 1955), p. 242.

6. Gail Thain Parker, "Jonathan Edwards and Melancholy" in <u>The New England Quarterly</u>, 41 (1968): 199.

7. Edwards, <u>Treatise on the Religious Affections</u>, ed. by John E. Smith (New Haven: Yale University Press, 1959), p. 189.

8. Edwards, <u>A Faithful Narrative of Surprising Conversions</u> in <u>The Works of Jonathan Edwards</u> (London: Banner of Truth Press, 1979), 1:353.

9. <u>Ibid.</u>, 1:353.

10. Normal Fiering, <u>Jonathan Edwards' Moral Thought and Its British Context</u> (Chapel Hill: University of North Carolina Press, 1981), p. 160.

11. Edwards' sensitivity to the problem of melancholic self-depreciation informs his hell-fire sermon <u>Sinners in the Hands of an Angry God</u>, often thought to be more harsh than it is. Through out his career, Edwards was critical of those who were swept away by "legal distresses" or the recognition of their justified condemnation, and failed to appreciate the "merciful God." In his famous sermon, Edwards did indeed seek to impress sinners with the wrath of God, but not at the expense of the virtue of hope. Conrad Cherry is especially sensitive to this balance between resignation and hope in his comments on Edwards' sermons:

> And running through these many sermons which on the surface are concerned exclusively with God's wrath, is a proclamation of the merciful God whose wrath yet burns toward sin. There is in "Sinners in the Hands of an Angry God," the sermon so often taken as representative of Edwards' pathological preoccupation with a God of wrath, a stream of hope and mercy running through the exposition of the wrath of God. <u>If</u> God should withdraw his hand, the sinner would fall into destruction. <u>If</u> God should let the sinful man go, . . . (See Conrad Cherry, <u>op. cit.</u>, p. 69)

Cherry argues that this hypothetical "if" mitigates the severity of Edwards' image of the sinner as a spider held over an open fire.

12. Edwards, <u>Charity and Its Fruits</u> (London: Banner of Truth Press, 1978), pp. 131-132.

13. <u>Ibid.</u>, p. 159.

14. <u>Ibid.</u> As early as 1732, Edwards articulated his adherence to this Augustinianism of his forebears:

> Love to God. Self-love. Whether or no a

man ought to love God more than himself. Self-love, taken in its most extensive sense, love to God, are not things properly capable of being compared with one another; for they are not opposites or things entirely distinct, but one enters into the nature of the other.

And he added, in the same note, that "the more a man loves God, the more unwilling will he be to be deprived of happiness." (See "Miscellany 530" in Townsend ed., The Philosophy of Jonathan Edwards, p. 202-203.

15. Edwards, Charity and Its Fruits , p. 268.

16. Ibid., p. 269.

17. Ibid., p. 270.

18. Ibid., pp. 271-272.

19. Ibid., p. 275.

20. In his Treatise on Religious Affections, for example, Edwards wrote, "Hope is so great a part of true religion, that the Apostle says we are saved by hope" (Rom. 8:24) (See p. 103) Hope is "one of the three great things of which religion consists" (1 Cor. 13:13); and is "an helmet, the hope of salvation." (See pp. 103-104) And the role of hope in the regenerate life is equally manifest in Edwards' Pressing into the Kingdom of God. Here he maintained that the Christian is to seek the kingdom and avoid "needless distresses that hey had much better do without." Rather than struggle with the resignatio ad infernum, one ought to be filled with personal hope. Without such hope, "it is thus very often with persons overrun with the distemper of melancholy; whence the adversary of souls is want to take great advantage." (See Works,

1:655) To cite another example, in <u>Ruth's Resolution</u>, Edwards continued to develop the theme of hope:

> Consider how earnestly desirous they that have obtained are that you should follow them, and that their people should be your people, and their God your God. They desire that you should partake of that great good which God has given them, and that unspeakable and eternal blessedness which he has promised them. (See <u>Works</u>, 1:667)

The regenerate desire that the reprobate join them in the assurance of "unspeakable and eternal blessedness."

21. John Locke, <u>An Essay Concerning Human Understanding</u>, ed. by John W. Yolton, 2 vols. (London: J.M. Dent and Sons, Ltd., 1961 ed.) 1:207. Henry Stob in "The Ethics of Jonathan Edwards" in <u>Faith and Philosophy</u>, ed. by Alvin P. Lantinga (Grand Rapids: William B. Eerdmans, 1968), clarifies Locke's influence on Edwards.

22. <u>Ibid.</u>, 1:213.

23. <u>Ibid.</u>

24. <u>Ibid.</u>, 1:220.

25. Edwards, <u>The Nature of True Virtue</u>, with a forward by William K. Frankena (Ann Arbor, MI: University of Michigan Press, 1960), p. 101.

26. Locke, 1:219.

27. Edwards, <u>Charity and Its Fruits</u>, p. 160.

28. <u>Ibid.</u>, p. 132.

29. For a useful analysis of covenant theologian

Johannes Wollebius and his impact on Edwards, see William S. Morris, "The Young Jonathan Edwards: A Reconstruction," (unpublished doctoral dissertation, University of Chicago, 1956).

30. Edwards, An Essay on the Trinity, ed. by Paul Helm, Treatise in Grace and Other Posthumously Published Writings (Cambridge: James Clarke and Co., 1971), p. 99.

31. Ibid., p. 103.

32. Ibid.

33. Ibid., p. 105.

34. Ibid.

35. Ibid.

36. Ibid.

37. The notion of God as suffering until the response of man brings him happiness was foreign to Edwards' system. God does not communicate happiness because his own well-being requires that of his creatures. As Douglass J. Elwood writes respecting Edwards, his philosophical theology was not that of "surrelativism" in which "God depends upon the world of contingencies for the completion of his being." Rather, "God is happy in himself in his relationship with his Son and the image internal to the Godhead." Elwood succinctly states it:

> At this point Edwards would have parted company with Charles Hartshorne and A.N. Whitehead, and the brand of panentheism sometimes called "surrelativism," according to which God depends upon the world of contingencies for the completion of his

being. There may be, Edwards would say, unactualized potentialities in the depth of the being of God, but there is nothing left to be desired which creation can add to his being. (See Douglass J. Elwood, The Philosophical Theology of Jonathan Edwards, (New York: Columbia University Press, 1960), p. 95.

God, then, is essentially complete and happy in the relationship between Father and the Son from eternity. God's happiness is in the trinitarian relationship, not in the relationship with mankind.

38. Why does God communicate this happiness? In Miscellany 699, Edwards responded in the following words:

Glory of God. God don't seek His own glory for any happiness He receives by it, as men are gratified in having their excellencies gazed at, admired, and extolled by others; but God seeks the display of his own glory as a thing in itself excellent. The display of the divine glory is that which is most excellent. Tis good that glory should be displayed. (See Edwards, The Philosophy of Edwards, ed. by Harvey G. Townsend (Eugene: University of Oregon Press, 1955), p. 139.

God sees his own happiness displayed in the happiness of his creatures, and this act of communication is in itself "excellent." God does not receive anything from the creature's happiness, except in the sense that he "would be less happy if He were less holy, or were capable of being hindered from any act of holiness . . . ."

Clearly the motive behind God's communication of happiness was important to Edwards. His fundamental argument was that God does not receive anything from such communication, and is the exemplar of a "love which seeketh not its own." Were God to benefit from the happiness of the creature, then an element of self-concern would enter into his communication. Edwards reiterated this point often:

> 679. Goodness of God. Love of God. Happiness of Heaven. God stands in no need of creatures and is not profited by them . . . As He delights in His own goodness, so He delights in the exercise of His goodness, and therefore He delights in exercising goodness or communicating happiness. (See Ibid., p. 139)

God's love is entirely disinterested, for were it otherwise, it would detract from the pure spontaneity of his goodness.

Edwards also reflected on God's communication of happiness in his The End For Which God Created the World, written as a companion piece to True Virtue. This treatise affirms the perfect happiness of God independent of creation as follows:

> 1. That no notion of God's last end in the creation of the world, is agreeable to reason, which would truly imply any indigence, insufficiency, and mutability in God; or any dependence of the Creator on the creature, for any part of his perfection or happiness. Because it is evident, by both Scripture and reason, that God is infinitely, eternally, unchangeably, and independently glorious and happy: that he cannot be profited by, or receive anything from, the creature; or be subject of any sufferings, or diminution of his glory and felicity, from any other being. (See Edwards, A Dissertation Concerning the End for Which God Created the World in Works, 1:97.)

Here Edwards reiterated his conviction as to the aseity of God, i.e., his absolute independence and self-contained happiness.

God's end, then, in creating the world, was not

to further his own happiness, but to emanate it. Edwards wrote that:

> Therefore, to speak strictly according to truth, we may suppose, that a disposition in God, as an original property of His nature, to an emanation of His own infinite fullness, was what excited him to create the world; and so, that the emanation itself was aimed at by him as a last end of the creation. (See Ibid., p. 100)

39. Edwards, Treatise on Grace in Treatise on Grace and Other Posthumously Published Writings (Cambridge: James Clarke and Co., 1971), p. 66.

40. Edwards, Charity and Its Fruits, p. 174.

41. Ibid., pp.172-173.

42. Ibid., p. 174.

43. Ibid.

44. Ibid.

45. Ibid.

46. Edwards, A Treatise Concerning Religious Affections, ed. by John E. Smith, Works of Jonathan Edwards (New Haven: Yale University Press, 1959), p. 240.

47. Ibid., p. 240.

48. Ibid.

49. Ibid., p. 241.

50. Ibid.

51. Ibid., p. 251.

52. Monroe C. Beardsley, Aesthetics From Classical Greece to the Present: A Short History (Birmingham: University of Alabama Press, 1966), p. 181.

53. Ibid. Taken from Shaftesbury's Characteristics.

54. Ibid.

55. Arthur Cushman McGiffert, Jr., Jonathan Edwards (New York: Harper and Brothers, 1932), p. 183. Cushman concludes thus:

> Most people pray for profit. They seek some reward by serving him. Nevertheless, there are, in addition to those who worship God because he is good to them, others who worship him because he is good in himself. The saint, the connoisseur in religion, loves God for his own sake. His is an 'unmercenary love of duty.' With both these attitudes Edwards was familiar. 'The grace of God may appear lovely in two ways: either as bonum utile, a profitable good to me, that which greatly serves my interest and so suits my self-love; or as a bonum formosum, a beautiful good in itself.' He had no doubts in his own mind as to which was the more truly religious attitude. (See p. 79)

56. Norman Fiering alludes to the significance of aesthetic theory in Edwards' thought, and makes several references to the importance of the influence of Hutcheson. Fiering writes that:

> It is in this context that the analogy with aesthetic experience, which Edwards embraced, is especially fruitful. We do not love a beautiful sunset or the glimmering

refulgence of the sunlight on green fields because of previous benefits bestowed or benefits expected. The response to beauty is involuntary and disinterested. A holy love to God, then, must be clearly distinguished from the kind that arises when there is a "preconceived relation" between the agent who loves and the object of that love, such as exists in family relations typically or in one's self-sacrificing regard for the welfare of groups that one to. Self-love (simple or compounded) is actually operative in these latter cases, Edwards believed, for there is usually some benefit already received or depended on.

Hutcheson, argues Fiering, provided Edwards with a framework from which to maintain that love for God can truly begin with God, and not from self-love. See Fiering, Jonathan Edwards's Moral Thought, p. 165.

57. Edwards, A Treatise Concerning Religious Affections, p. 246.

58. Edwards, Treatise on Grace in Treatise on Grace and Other Posthumously Published Writings, ed. Paul Helm (Cambridge: James Clarke and Co., 1971), pp. 50-51.

59. Edwards, A Treatise Concerning Religious Affections, p. 242.

60. Ibid.

61. Ibid., p. 242.

62. Ibid., footnote 5.

63. Ibid., p. 248.

64. <u>Ibid.</u>, pp. 248-249.

65. Edwards, <u>The Nature of True Virtue</u>, p. 8.

66. <u>Ibid.</u>

67. <u>Ibid.</u>, p. 11.

68. <u>Ibid.</u>, p. 89.

69. <u>Ibid.</u>, p. 92.

70. <u>Ibid.</u>, p. 101.

Chapter IV

Samuel Hopkins: A New Departure

Samuel Hopkins' concept of disinterested benevolence is consistent with the piety of radical self-denial that emerged in the late seventeenth century both in Europe and in New England. While Edwards rejected the radical alternative for reasons already discussed, Hopkins embraced it. More than any American of his period, Hopkins was, like Fénelon, a disciple of fully disinterested love.

Hopkins' uncompromising polemic against self-love in any of its guises moved beyond Fénelon's concern with the question of love for God, by encompassing love for neighbor as well, though he by no means abandoned this characteristically seventeenth-century concern. He translated the ideal of pure love for God into a vigorously self-denying social ethic. Departing from Edwards' suspicion of radical self-denial, Hopkins stressed God and neighbor as the objects of radically self-denying love, precluding love of self even in

Edwards' carefully defined sense of consent to all being including one's own. Hopkins built his ethic, then, on careful revisions of his mentor Edwards' thought.[1]

The ideal of self-denial articulated by Hopkins contributed to antebellum Protestant reform. Charles Finney, one of the most prolific revivalist-reformers, developed an ethic somewhat consistent with Hopkinsianism, maintaining that the regenerate are "totally unselfish or totally altruistic."[2] William McLoughlin quotes Finney thus ". . . all sin consists in selfishness, and all holiness or virtue in disinterested benevolence."[3] The ethic of radical self-denial, insofar as it was embedded in the Second Great Awakening, was, as McLoughlin mentions, "feared by the conservative New England revivalists; nevertheless, after 1830 it came to dominate American social thought."[4] Self-effacing altruism transcends the distinction between required moral acts and acts of supererogation. Public life became the testing ground for self-denial which knew no limits.

Though Hopkinsianism too thoroughly opposed all regard for one's own welfare, it served an important strategic purpose. Edwards' insistence on proper consent to oneself may not have allowed for the radically self-denying idealism helpful in this inspiration of serious social activism. As Alexander V. G. Allen commented in 1891, while Hopkinsianism calls for a self-denial "beyond the power of endurance" and to the ordinary view, "an act of spiritual suicide," it nevertheless proved inspirational and socially efficacious.[5] Allen cites the following enthusiastic comment on Hopkins' ethic made by a convert to his teachings, Mrs. Sedgwick of Newport: ". . . that most ennobling doctrine of Hopkinsianism, complete self-abnegation—a total regard and consecration to the glory of the Creator."[6]

A New Definition of Disinterested Benevolence

In the late 1780's Hopkins wrote his <u>A Dialogue Between a Calvinist and a Semi-Calvinist</u>. Foster writes that "the intensely earnest and radical spirit of Hopkinsianism appears here more clearly, perhaps, than anywhere else."[7] Written as a response to critics of the doctrine of the willingness to be damned—Hopkins articulation of the medieval <u>resignatio ad infernum</u>—the <u>Dialogue</u> was published posthumously and gained popularity. It is the most precise statement of Hopkins' unmitigated commitment to the pure love tradition, and thus merits careful attention.

Hopkins was convinced that his theology was consistent with that of Calvin, and referred to his emphasis on submission to God's will rather than on reconciliation with God as true to the Genevan reformer. Calvin did argue that one ought not to try to discern God's mysterious decrees—in effect, one ought not to be concerned with assurance of personal salvation—but he at no point adopted the doctrine of <u>resignatio ad infernum</u>. The demand that one must be willing to "perish forever" for God's glory is really an interpretation of Calvinism which could only emerge after the seventeenth-century pure love controversy. The <u>Dialogue</u> is thematically similar to Fénelon's <u>A Dissertation on Pure Love</u>.

In the <u>Dialogue</u>, the Calvinist is pitted against the Semi-Calvinist. The latter questions the doctrine of the willingness to be damned as had Willard and Edwards:

> Semi-Calvinist. Sir, I have wanted, for sometime to talk with you about the notion which some lately advance, viz., that Christians may, yea, that they ought, and must, be willing to perish forever, in order to be Christians. This is a shocking doctrine

to me; for I believe it absolutely impossible for any one to be willing to be eternally wretched; and if it were possible, it would be very wicked; for we are contrary to this, viz., to desire and seek to escape damnation, and to be saved; as all our most considerable and best divines have taught, which I could easily prove, were it necessary.[8]

This Semi-Calvinist criticism is essentially the voice of New England orthodoxy whose proponents disputed Hopkins' interpretation of Calvinism.

Hopkins responded to this criticism through the voice of his Calvinist. He admits that the willingness to be damned is, taken alone, highly suspect. It would then be an end in itself, serving no higher purpose, and chosen "for its own sake."[9] Self-abnegation is not an ideal of Christianity so much as a necessity. In so arguing, Hopkins cited Paul's passage in Romans 9:3, "I could wish myself accursed from Christ, for my brethren, . . ."[10] To be willing to be damned is "to prefer a greater good to a less" if thereby God's glorious Kingdom will be established on earth. In citing Romans 9, Hopkins was consistent with Abelard, Luther, Fénelon, and others who refused to let the Augustinian view that love seeks the true well-being of the lover pass unchallenged.

In response to the Semi-Calvinist argument that it is impossible to will one's own damnation, the Calvinist maintains that to be willing to suffer eternal misery is not to actively desire it. Rather, one obediently acknowledges God's sovereignty.[11] It is this passive concurrence which supposedly retrieves Hopkins' position from the criticism that it fosters self-destruction. Edwards, of course, would not have been satisfied with this response, given his polemic against melancholy and his emphasis on personal hope. Hopkins himself certainly thought that the appeal to passive concurrence undermines the Semi-Calvinist critique.

The themes of self-denial as a means to a higher end and of passive concurrence are evident in passages from the Dialogue's Calvinist such as this:

> You know that it is is most for the glory of God that some should be damned. And if you do not know that you are a Christian, you do not know but it is in fact true that it is most for the glory of God that you should be damned; the supposition is therefore natural and easy, and you cannot well avoid making it. Supposing, then, this were true, which may be true, notwithstanding anything you know, how ought you to feel with respect to it? Ought you not to be willing to be damned.[12]

The willingness to be damned articulated here was so characteristic of Hopkins' theology that by the early 1800's it was, as McLoughlin notes, known as "the 'willingness to be damned' concept of conversion."[13] Not to concur with damnation was viewed as un-Christian. To assume, argued Hopkins through his Calvinist, that God will make one "entirely happy at last" is to express nothing but selfishness, in making God a tool to answer our own selfish ends."[14] It is necessary for the Christian to unconditionally place him or herself in God's hands. Happiness is not a Christian moral end, and all self-love should be thoroughly expunged from the Christian ethic. Hopkins sought to disentangle pure love for God from any self-regarding impulses—in short, he sought to undo New England Augustinianism. Though its style is ponderous, the Dialogue is an impressive statement of an important aspect of the New England mind.

Related to Hopkins' theme of the willingness to be damned is his rejection of Edwards' complex theological anthropology which combines "natural" and "divine" principles. The two-story Edwardsian anthropology contradicts the radical self-denial which Hopkins called for; such denial knows no compromise with the natural principle of self-love. Hopkins presented a one-story image of the regenerate in his <u>An Inquiry Into the Nature of True Holiness</u>, published in 1773.

In <u>True Holiness</u>, Hopkins defined holiness as a single principle or affection. To achieve such a simplification, Hopkins began with the question "What is God's moral character?"[15] To know this is to understand the holiness of the regenerate, for the saints' moral character differs not in kind but only in degree from that of God. As Hopkins put it, "Holiness in God is not different, in nature and kind, from the holiness of creatures."[16]

Holiness in God consists, argued Hopkins, in the single affection of disinterested benevolence. This is exemplified by his giving his Son to die for sinners, God's "unreasonable and abusive enemies." Morever, God's character can be seen in Christ, for to know Christ is to know God. Christ is the "most striking instance of disinterested benevolence," experiencing the epitome of "unhappiness" that others might be saved. Like God, Christ "seeketh not his own;" to say that "God is love" is to describe God as "pure, disinterested benevolence." Contrary to the typical argument of Hopkins' period put forward by Jonathan Edwards among others, he held that God has "nothing of the nature of what is called self-love . . . ." In short, both God and Christ exercise disinterested affections which place no limit on self-denial. The holiness of men consists in imitating the benevolent love of God and Christ, as symbolized by the cross. Indeed, Hopkins virtually identifies Christian love with the crucifixion.

In placing the benevolence of God first in the ranks of divine attributes, Hopkins was in accord with a broad friend in late eighteenth century theology. In the 1750's Charles Chauncey and Jonathan Mayhew, to note just two examples, published important treatises on the theme of divine benevolence. As Conrad Wright put its,

"They became profoundly convinced that God is a benevolent deity whose first concern is the happiness of his creatures."[17] Wright points out that Chauncey and others were "combating the tendency of high Calvinism to make the gulf between God and man so wide that human concepts, when applied to the deity, lose their familiar meaning."[18] But Hopkins went far beyond these liberal Arminians in associating benevolence with thorough renunciation of self-love.

The holiness of the saint is identical in kind with that of God, argued Hopkins, because it is of divine origin. It is a "participation of the divine" in the creature. Holiness descends from above, and has no relationship with mere human nature. Hence, Willard's and Edwards' insistence that God works in accordance with human nature created as good is undermined. Edwards' sense of what is psychologically possible for human nature was foreign to Hopkins. As a result, the latter emphasized the "simplicity" of the state of holiness in which disinterested love alone, prevails, and is not entangled with the natural principle which Edwards included in his image of Christian virtue. As Hopkins wrote,

> True holiness is in its own nature one simple, uncompounded thing. It is not made up of different and various kinds of exercises, properties and ingredients, which may exist distinct and separate, or in any degree independent of each other, and being put together make one compound' . . . [19]

This definition of holiness served a polemic purpose against other theories of virtue propounded by New England theologians. On the one hand, argued Hopkins, some hold the natural principle of self-love to be the "spring of all our actions," while others view self-love as "innocent by nature," though in need of regulation. A third alternative, affirmed by Hopkins, is that self-love is "no part of holiness, but opposed to it."[20] Edwards rejected the first of these alternatives, but like Stoddard before him accepted the second. Hopkins would have nothing to do with this second alternative, replete with its "superstructure" of self-love. As he stated in uncompromising manner, "self-love is, in its whole nature, and in every degree of it, enmity against God. It is not subject to the law of God, nor indeed can be; and is the only affection that can oppose it.[21]

Hopkins was convinced that the opposition between holiness and all self-love is Scripturally warranted. Disinterested benevolence contrasts with a love which "always seeks its own and nothing else."[22] To be willing to suffer damnation is the epitome of disinterestedness, it is to "say with Moses, 'Blot me, I pray thee, out of thy book.'"[23]

Like Moses, the saint acknowledges that "if my salvation is inconsistent with this, I give all up, I have no interest of my own to seek or desire."[24] The saint can have no self-love because Scripture indicates that all love of self is never a "harmless creature," but always "a devouring beast of prey."[25]

In addition to his reference to Moses, Hopkins made extensive use of Luke 6:32 in interpreting the command to love God. In his <u>System of Doctrines</u> published in 1793, he wrote:

We hence learn how false and pernicious that doctrine is, which too many have held and asserted, namely, that true love for God originates from a knowledge or belief that he loves us, and designs to make us happy; or that a man cannot love God, unless he first has evidence that God loves him with a design to save him. This is excluding dis-interested affection entirely, and making all religious affection to consist in self-love; for that love to any being which is wholly owing to a knowledge or belief that he loves us, is nothing but self-love. Our Savior, therefore,

condemns this, as not true Christian love,
but a love which He says, "if ye love them
which love you, what thank have ye? For
sinners also love those that love them."
(Luke vi. 32) [26]

The polemic use of Luke 6:32 against those who
hold all love to be rooted in self-concern is central
to Hopkins' argument. [27] It issues in the following
proscription:

He who has a new heart, and universal
disinterested benevolence, will be a friend to
God, and must be pleased with his infinitely
benevolent character, though he see not the
least evidence, and has not a thought that
God loves him and intends to save him.[28]

This is an adequate summary of what Hopkins'
thought scripture requires.

Hopkins' notion of Christian love is problematic
in its emphasis on radical self-denial; it defined the
state of holiness in a manner that jettisons all
self-love; it identifies Christian love with the cross;
it allows no place for the theological virtue of hope;
and it fails to consider the psychological realities of
human nature. In short, it requires the Christian to
surrender participation in the mutual good of
communion with God and neighbor. Yet it found a
role in the American social context nevertheless.

Hopkins' Ethic in Social Context

Noted American political historian Gordon S.
Wood has defined republicanism as the "sacrifice of
individual interests to the greater good of the whole
. . "[29] According to Wood, this was "the idealistic
goal of the Revolution." Of course many Americans shared this ideal despite philosophical
differences. Thomas Paine, for instance, referred to
the classic Greek republic as a society concerned

with the public good rather than the good of a sovereign.[30]   Wood is careful to include New England Protestantism in his list of contributors to the republican vision.   He cites the example of a sermon preached by Phillip Payson in 1798 in Boston which reads thus:

> The representatives of the people would not act as spokesmen for private and partial interests, but all would be 'disinterested men, who could have no interest of their own to seek,' and 'would employ their whole time for the public good; then there would be but one interest, the good of the people of large.'[31]

The most cursory reading of the Protestant literature of the post-Revolutionary period provides ample evidence that disinterested benevolence came to be identified with republican ideals.   Even prior to the Revolution, as Wood remarks, "Independence thus became not only political but moral.   Revolution, republicanism, and regeneration all blended in American thinking."[32]   The "light of nature and revelation" were "firmly united," such that "Religion and republicanism would work hand in hand to create frugality, honesty, self-denial, and benevolence among the people."[33]   Liberal rationalism and "Calvinist Christian love" created a common emphasis on the general good.   As Samuel Adams put it, there would be a "Christian Sparta."[34]   Wood states, "Enlightened rationalism and evangelical Christianity were not at odds in 1776;" rather, "millennial Christianity and pagan classicism" shared a common vision.[35]   Many Protestant reform organizations of the antebellum period "fitted perfectly into the republican ideals of a virtuous citizenry sacrificing itself for the greater good of the community."[36]

It is easy to see the congruity of Hopkins' thought with republicanism.   Indeed, in his <u>System of</u>

<u>Doctrines</u>, written late in his career, he did politicize his theology to an extent. He identified the object of disinterested benevolence as "the public interest," in contrast to "private good." And he himself became especially active in the anti-slavery movement. David Brion Davis comments that Hopkins was ardent in the anti-slavery cause because of his definition of true virtue as an active, outgoing "disinterested benevolence toward mankind."[37]

One of Hopkins' most interesting socio-political works is his <u>Dialogue Concerning the Slavery of the Africans</u> (1776), dedicated to the Continental Congress. Bernard Bailyn maintains that Hopkins, among the new England Congregationalists, "had first come to see the social meaning of his doctrines of 'disinterested benevolence' and 'general atonement'" in the anti-slavery context.[38] Bailyn then proceeds to analyze the <u>Dialogue Concerning Slavery</u>, emphasizing its widespread influence. The <u>Dialogue</u> was undoubtedly a groundbreaking treatise because it displays the activist reform orientation that would permeate Hopkinsianism and the Second Awakening. Its influence on all levels of American intellectual life was due to its wide distribution by the "Society for Promoting the Manumission of Slaves," formed in 1785 in New York and headed by John Jay. The Society ordered 2,000 copies of the <u>Dialogue</u> and was responsible for several reprintings.[39] It provided copies to all the members of the United States' Congress, as well as to New York's State legislators.[40]

In the <u>Dialogue</u>, the slaves are depicted as oppressed and helpless. America stands "under the divine judgements for this sins of enslaving the Africans."[41] Concern for the oppressed is a sign of truly disinterested affections, as well as a sense of the justice that benevolence implies. The Old Testament prophets play a role in the <u>Dialogue</u>, as well as in the slightly later <u>An Address to the</u>

77

<u>Owners of Negroe Slaves in the American Colonies</u>. In the latter, Zachariah and Ezekiel are mentioned as champions of the widow, the fatherless, the stranger, and the poor. Hopkins asked "Are not the African slaves among the oppressed?"[42] To care for the slaves was to oppose injustice and provided the measure for holiness. Armed with these ideas, Hopkins was remarkably successful in turning the ministers and legislators in Rhode Island and other areas of New England against slavery.[43]

The emphasis on self-denying benevolence coincided with the vision of the earthly millennium to place Hopkins and Hopkinsians in the forefront of reform movements. Hopkins predicted the precise character of the society which would gradually emerge through Christian reform efforts prior to the return of Christ. In his <u>A Treatise on the Millennium,</u> he envisions an age of disinterested benevolence in which those in need will be relieved, there will be a tremendous increase in scientific knowledge and technology, war will be abolished and a universal language will facilitate communication."[44]

Hopkins began his <u>Treatise</u> with an astute recognition of the popularity of "the doctrine of the Millennium" in the first "three centuries after the Apostles." But, "so many unworthy and absurd things were by some advanced concerning it, that it afterwards fell into discredit . . ."[45] Though it was revived with the Reformation, the doctrine was again discredited by misuse until Whitby, Lowman, and "the late President Edwards" gave it new credibility, such that "the doctrine of the millennium is now better understood and believed."[46] He then attempted to interpret <u>Revelation</u> 20:1-6. Hopkins opposed the literal interpretation that Jesus will return "in his human nature" to set up his Kingdom on earth, reigning "visibly, and personally." Rather <u>Revelation</u> 20 must be understood "in a figurative sense." It does not mean that

Christ will reign visibly, but will subdue "all hearts to a willing subjection" and overthrow "the kingdom of Satan."[47] By a "new heaven and a new earth" is meant the "renovation of the hearts of men by the Spirit of God" through Christ's "spiritual power." In short, there will be a "spiritual resurrection, a resurrection of the souls of the whole church on earth."[48]

The millennium will be a time of true holiness, of a disinterested benevolence that will "banish all the evils which have existed and prevailed in the world."[49] All social oppression will cease. And because knowledge and holiness are "inseparably connected," there will be "great advances" in the arts and sciences.[50] Animal husbandry will be developed, the technical or "mechanic arts" will be applied to the cultivation of the earth such that it will bear fruit "one hundred fold more."[51] All "outward circumstances" will prosper allowing leisure time for study, and modern utensils will be available for all. Mankind will "greatly multiply" to fill the earth in accord with Genesis 1:28, "be fruitful, multiply, and replenish, (or fill) the earth, and subdue it."[52] All of this will occur "almost two hundred years from the end of this present century," or about the year 2000, though the millennium will be brought about through the dutiful activism of the Church in the immediate present.[53]

Hopkins, then, provided material content to the millennium in an unprecedented manner, and was one of the fathers of American social utopianism. The power of his millennium vision (in concert with is doctrine of love) was tremendous. Oliver Elsbree writes that the doctrine of disinterested benevolence along with an ardent post-millennialism was sufficient to inspire scores of young American Hopkinsians "with a fanatical enthusiasm for becoming America's first mission-aries to Asia."[54] As they began to evangelize the world starting in 1812, they felt "swallowed up in the well-being of the universe."[55]

The social value of Hopkins' evangelical ethics has often been lost sight of because, as Timothy L. Smith points out, "since 1890 mass evangelism has often been associated with theologically obscurantist and socially negative religion . . . "[56] Students of American social thought thus might neglect the pervasive connection between religion and social transformation. But as one sociologist has written, "The experience of sanctification socialized the individual disposition and released in men the mystic power to make benevolent motives work."[57] For Hopkinsians, to be sanctified meant social activism, while to be uninterested in benevolent enterprises was evidence of a "back-slidden heart." A true Christian was to be a reformer indifferent to one's own well-being and a harbinger of the holy millennial-republic.

The Errors of Hopkinsianism

Nathan Bangs published his The Errors of Hopkinsianism in 1815.[58] Bangs, a New York City minister, was frustrated by the prevalence of Hopkinsian doctrine in the "burned-over" revival areas of upstate New York. Bangs was an anti-Hopkinsian crusader frequently engaging in public debates on Hopkinsian theology which he considered dangerous and confused.

In particular, Bangs was alarmed at Hopkins' notion of disinterested benevolence. He held that God promises "the happiness of all intelligent creatures," and that "the glory of God, and the happiness of men are two points, which ultimately concentrate, and in practice can never be separated."[59] Bangs insisted that to talk about "abstracting ourselves, so as to have no regard to our own happiness, is an ideal theory, having no foundation in scripture, and is utterly repugnant to common sense."[60] True, he argued, "worldly lust" is to be denied, but such denial is not made "without any regard to our present and eternal happiness."[61] The Hopkinsian doctrine "declares that a man must be willing to be damned." Bangs held that "it is utterly impossible for a man to be actuated by such a principle," for to "have no interest in a thing is to be wholly indifferent to it," and without an interest in personal well-being there is no reason to act morally.[62] A self-less motive is "beyond the reach of man." Even God seeks "his own glory, in all his works and ways." God promises rewards "to incite the Christian to diligence in running the race set before him."[63]

The thrust of Bangs' polemic is one which is difficult to reject: in order for the Christian to love God and do good, there must be an element of self-love in the Christian ethic. To have "no interest" whatsoever in self—Bangs' definition of "disinterestedness"—is to acquiesce in a condition of passivity. While Hopkins and other proponents of pure love do appear to have been wrong in what they said about love, the sheer motivating power of Hopkins' thought and its perennial attractiveness is clear. As Park wrote in his Memoir,

> If Hopkins had adorned his sentiments with the graces of poetic style, he would have been a favorite with those imaginative writers who lose themselves in the praise of a self-sacrificing spirit, of a self-forgetful soul, swallowed up in the well-being of the unwise.[64]

Thus, while the Hopkinsian ethic of radical self-denial misrepresents the Christian ideal, as the next chapter emphasizes, its inspirational value must be acknowledged.

Footnotes

1. I disagree with Joseph Conforti's thesis that Hopkins was primarily reacting against the possessive individualism of Yankee mercantilism and "self-love" ethical theories. Certainly Hopkins opposed these developments, but the roots of his thought lie in the pure love alternative in the wider historical tradition of Christian theology. His <u>A Dialogue Between a Calvinist and a Semi-Calvinist</u>, for instance, was not a politically motivated tract; it was a response to critics of his notion of the willingness to be damned for the glory of God. (See Conforti, p. 120; and Foster's <u>A Genetic History of New England Theology</u>, p. 156).

2. William G. McLoughlin, <u>Revivals, Awakenings, and Reform</u> (Chicago: University of Chicago Press, 1978), pp. 128-9.

3. <u>Ibid.</u>, p. 129.

4. <u>Ibid.</u>

5. Alexander V. G. Allen, "The Transition in New England Theology," <u>Atlantic Monthly</u> 68 (December, 1891) : 767-80, p. 776.

6. <u>Ibid.</u>

7. Frank Hugh Foster, <u>A History of the New England Theology</u> (Chicago: University of Chicago Press, 1907).

8. Samuel Hopkins, <u>A Dialogue Between a Calvinist and a Semi-Calvinist</u> in <u>The Works of Samuel Hopkins</u> (Boston: Doctrinal Tract and Book Society, 1854 edition), 3:143.

9. <u>Ibid.</u>, 144.

10. _Ibid._

11. Lee Osborne Scott, "The Concept of Love as Universal Disinterested Benevolence in the Early Edwardseans," (Doctoral Dissertation: Yale University, 1952), p. 322, uses the expression "passive state of concurrence."

12. Hopkins, _Dialogue,_ 3:147.

13. William G. McLoughlin, p.101.

14. Hopkins, _Dialogue,_ 3:157.

15. Hopkins, _An Inquiry into the Nature of True Holiness_ (Newport: Solomon Southwick, 1773), p. iii.

16. _Ibid.,_ p. 3.

17. Conrad Wright, _The Beginnings of Unitarianism in America_ (Boston: Starr King Press, 1955), p. 161.

18. _Ibid.,_ p. 172.

19. Hopkins, _True Holiness,_ p. 4.

20. _Ibid.,_ p. 19.

21. _Ibid.,_ p. 28.

22. _Ibid.,_ p. 58.

23. _Ibid.,_ p. 74.

24. _Ibid._

25. _Ibid.,_ p. 26.

26. Hopkins, <u>System of Doctrines</u> in <u>Works of Samuel Hopkins</u>, 1:388.

27. <u>Ibid.</u>, 1:390.

28. <u>Ibid.</u>, 1:389.

29. Gordon S. Wood, <u>The Creation of the American Republic 1776-1787</u> (Chapel Hill: University of North Carolina Press, 1969), p. 53.

30. <u>Ibid.</u>, p. 56.

31. <u>Ibid.</u>, p. 59.

32. <u>Ibid.</u>, p. 117.

33. <u>Ibid.</u>, p. 118.

34. <u>Ibid.</u>

35. <u>Ibid.</u>, p. 60.

36. William G. McLoughlin, p. 113.

37. David Brion Davis, <u>The Problem of Slavery in Western Culture</u> (Ithaca, New York: Cornell University Press, 1966), pp. 371; and on Hopkins and anti-slavery, see also Winthrop D. Jordan, <u>White over Black: American Attitudes Toward the Negro, 1550-1812</u> (New York: W.W. Norton and Company, Inc., 1968).

38. Bernard Bailyn, <u>The Ideological Origins of the American Revolution</u> (Cambridge: Harvard University Press, 1967), p. 243.

39. See Hopkins, <u>A Dialogue Concerning the Slavery of Africans</u> (New York: reprinted for R.

Hodge, 1785), p. 4 of the introductory letters from the Society for the Manumission of Slaves.

40. See Joseph Conforti, p. 136.

41. Hopkins, <u>A Dialogue Concerning the Slavery of African</u>, p. 12.

42. <u>Ibid.</u>, from <u>An Address to the Owners of Negroe Slaves in the American Colonies</u>, p. 65.

43. Hopkins' plan for the colonization of freed slaves in Africa is developed in a variety of his other writings. See Conforti, Ch. 9. Conforti documents the impact of Hopkins' anti-slavery agitation in detail.

44. See Ernest Lee Tuveson, <u>Redeemer Nation: The Idea of America's Millennial Role</u> (Chicago: University of Chicago Press, Midway Reprint, 1968) pp. 60-63.

45. Hopkins, <u>A Treatise on the Millennium</u> (Boston: Printed by Isaiah Thomas and Ebenezer T. Andrews, 1793), p. 6.

46. <u>Ibid.</u>, p. 7.

47. <u>Ibid.</u>, p. 43.

48. <u>Ibid.</u>, p. 12.

49. <u>Ibid.</u>, p. 56.

50. <u>Ibid.</u>, p. 58.

51. <u>Ibid.</u>, p. 71.

52. <u>Ibid.</u>, pp. 73-74.

53. Ibid., p. 98.

54. Oliver Wendell Elsbree, "Samuel Hopkins and His Doctrine of Benevolence," in New England Quarterly 8(1935); 534-41, 541.

55. Edwards A. Park in Memoir, Works of Samuel Hopkins, 1:211.

56. Timothy L. Smith, Revivalism and Social Reform: American Protestantism on the Eve of the Civil War (New York: Harper and Row, 1957), p. 46.

57. William J. Warner, cited by Timothy L. Smith, pp. 160-1.

58. Nathan Bangs, The Errors of Hopkinsianism Detected and Refuted in Six Letters (Bowery, New York: Printed by John C. Totton, 1815).

59. Ibid., p. 270.

60. Ibid., p. 271.

61. Ibid.

62. Ibid., p. 273.

63. Ibid., p. 276.

64. Edwards A. Park in Memoir, Works of Samuel Hopkins, 1:211.

Chapter V

The Meaning of Christian Love

In the communion of Christian love for God and neighbor, there is no place for self-love defined as the pursuit of one's own separate good outside of relationship. However, there is a place for self-love insofar as one must participate in the mutual good of communion, rather than surrender participation. A plain fact of human existence is the will to belong to community, for it is in communion that the self takes form and finds meaning. Edwards' recognition of the role of such love for self in communion is evident from his argument that sin "has its source from selfishness, or from self-love not subordinate to a regard to being in general." Self-love, subordinate to participation in the good of communion, is admissible in Edwards' view. Indeed, it is "exceedingly necessary."

Thus far in this text, a strain in the wider history of Christian ethical ideas which has had the unfortunate consequence of devaluing all self-love has been underscored in relation to its impact on the thought of Edwards and Hopkins. Edwards' appreciation for the role of true self-love has been highlighted because it is at this juncture that one branch of American reflection on the meaning of Christian love takes form.

"Two main interpretations of the meaning of Christian love," writes Paul Ramsey, "are contending for acceptance in present-day theological discussion."[1] On the one hand, there are those who hold that the primary meaning of love is to be found in self-denial; on the other are those who believe that community or "the highest and truest form of mutual love" is the ideal of Christian ethics.[2] The debate in theological ethics over the meaning of love remains a live one. While Ramsey argues that "self-sacrifice" captures "the more correct reading of biblical and New Testament ethics," this view is not above contention.[3] It can, I think, be persuasively argued that love is a two-term relation, presupposing the meeting of two in communion and unity. Here self-denial is an aspect of Christian love which is demanded primarily when community requires restoration. Christian love does not seek only the good of the beloved, but the good of community, all participants considered. The ideal of love is not merely to be a "long-distance runner moving through the dark."[4]

Within this framework, Edwards and Hopkins present disparate interpretations of the meaning of Christian love. For Edwards, a form of self-love "enters into the nature of love for God." Edwards writes of the consent of being to being, an image which leans heavily in the direction of communion and mutuality. Within God, contends Edwards, Father and Son share in a reciprocal relationship which results in an overflowing divine happiness imparted to the Christian through the Holy Spirit. Edwards' ideal of community emerges equally clearly in the sixteenth chapter of Charity and Its Fruits. "Love in heaven," writes Edwards, "is always mutual."[5] Moreover, "It is always met with answerable returns of love—with returns that are proportioned to its exercise."[6] The love of the saints, emphasizes Edwards, "will always be mutual and reciprocated."[7] As a result of this communion in love, the joy of heaven will "never be interrupted." Those who participate in it shall have "perfect enjoyment of each other's love."[8]

Hopkins, a stark contrast to Edwards, makes an idol of self-denial. His concern was not with the joy of perfect communion, but with the ideal of sacrifice. He presents American Protestantism with a form of disinterest or indifference to one's own well-being requiring nothing less than a chaotic surrender of self which violates the structures of personal and social existence as Edwards observed these. In short, Hopkins confuses the virtue of unselfishness which makes the joy and reciprocity of community possible with an arid selflessness.

In this chapter, my task is to critically assess some themes in the thought of Edwards and Hopkins with regard to the meaning of Christian love. In addition, I offer some constructive comments as to the direction in which I would like to see theological reflection on the idea of Christian love move.

Religious Experience and Self-Denial

The experience of the holy, Rudolf Otto writes, includes the feeling of "self-devaluation."[9] The person senses the absolute value of the deity, along with a corresponding realization of his or her own disvalue. In the effort to cleanse the self of its profanity, various of the great mystics have taken the ascetic path of self-denial. Not only have they denied themselves bodily satisfactions, for some have gone so far as to claim that "the satisfactions of the spirit must go the same way as the satisfactions of the senses."[10] Madame Guyon, Fénelon, and as mentioned previously, Mrs. Jonathan Edwards, exemplify this infatuation with indifference to self. The famous challenge of Samuel Hopkins, "Are you willing to be damned for the glory of God?", is an articulation of just this form of indifference. This quest for disinterestedness, as it emerges from religious experience, is invariably tied to the ethical doctrine of radically self-denying love for the neighbor.   Just as one denies oneself the satisfactions and joys which a relationship with the divine might otherwise bring, so also one refuses to receive love from the neighbor in communion. The self is absolutely negated in all aspects of human experience.

In contemporary American theological ethics, Paul Ramsey maintains that the "old Calvinistic test for candidates for the ministry, "Are you willing to be damned for the glory of God?' is, of course, totally unacceptable, even a repulsive, 'horrible decree,' for what it says about God."[11] But Ramsey immediately adds that "it would be difficult to frame a more succinct statement of the bearing of 'salvation' on Christian ethics."[12] For whoever is willing to be damned, contends Ramsey, is "truly saved—for his neighbor."[13] Such willingness, he insists, has "ethical consequences." Ramsey, who advocates the ideal of "disinterested" love throughout his Basic Christian Ethics—and "disinterested" is his preferred expression, indicating indebtedness to the history of American theological ideas—appreciates the Hopkinsian doctrine. Thus, a prominent figure on the American theological scene indicates the relationship between religious resignation in its extreme and selfless love of neighbor. Of course Ramsey's emphasis on conventanal love mitigates his stress on disinterestedness.

In all of this, however, Ramsey is more the heir of Hopkins than of Edwards. For Edwards has no

tolerance of that "old Calvinistic test" of which Ramsey writes. Rather, Edwards was convinced of the overflowing happiness which God communicates to soul—a happiness created through the community of Father and Son within the divine. Edwards, following the teachings of the Puritan Augustinians such as Ames and Stoddard, understood love for God as the possibility for personal fulfillment and ecstatic joy. Utter self-denial has no place in Edwards religious-ethical vision.

Having earlier indicated where Hopkins and Edwards depart with regard to self-denial in the light of religious experience, there are serious weaknesses in Hopkins' thought which need to be underlined. However much resignation is an ineradicable aspect of religious experience and ethical life, it ought not to be viewed as a final stage of perfection. The Old Testament figure Ezekiel teaches a lesson in this regard. He buried his face in the dirt whenever God appeared to him, until finally, in exasperation, God commands him "Man, stand up and let me talk to you." (Ezek. 2:1) Ezekiel learned that God himself wants communion rather than groveling. To make radical self-denial the center of gravity in discussions of love for God or neighbor is, then, to frustrate the final goal of all love, i.e., communion in which the self prospers with others.

Self-denial is, of course, one of the most important moral resources of religion. Insofar as egocentricity is transcended through the religious experience of the holy, allowing the self to be recentered in communion with God and others, such experience is the sine qua non of ethics. But in its extreme form, as an end in itself, resignation is counterproductive. It spells the absolute eclipse of communion as a viable definition of Christian love, leaving us with Fénelon's claim that, "We must wholly die to all friendship."

In the final analysis, radical self-denial condemns selfishness rather than encourages love. For love entails a relation between two or more selves, and to become preoccupied with inner purity is to ignore the actual flow of love between persons. Reinhold Niebuhr articulates this ambiguity as follows:

> It cannot be denied that mysticism and asceticism involve themselves in every kind of absurdity in the attempt to root out the selfishness of which their mystical contemplation has made them conscious. The mystic involves himself not only in the practical absurdity of becoming obsessed with self, in the very fever to eliminate it, but in the rational absurdity of passing judgment upon even the most unselfish desires as being selfish because they are desires.[14]

To be detached from all of one's desires for well-being is to achieve a state of stoical indifference rather than love. Judgment must be passed on egocentricity, and religious experience is where, in theocentric ethics, this judgment occurs. But after the judgment has passed, the self is freed for the ideal of true self-love in communion and unity. Those who advocate radical self-denial as the core feature of Christian love cannot take this ideal to heart.

The ambiguity of radical self-denial is captured succinctly by Walter Rauschenbusch, as well. Committed to an ideal of communion and mutuality, Rauschenbusch comments favorably on the Christian doctrine of self-sacrifice. Yet, he insists, it must not "take a man out of society" or annihilate natural impulses, for "Christ has once for all demonstrated the possible holiness of common human life."[15] Common human life, of course, is life lived in communion. To make disinterestedness the center of virtue is to devalue such communion. So too, Josiah Royce, in his discussion of "the idea of the universal community," writes that "the God who loves me demands not that I should be nothing, but that I should be his own."[16] However much the effort to purge egoism from the self provides support for the spirit of love as communion, such introspection can blind the Christian to the beauty of participation in the mutual good and the form of self-love this entails.

More recently, James M. Gustafson has considered the theme of self-denial in the light of theocentric piety. "A theocentric piety, I believe," writes Gustafson, "motivates and issues in a readiness to restrain particular interests for the sake of other persons, for communities and the larger world."[17] Acts which ordinarily would be seen as supererogatory are, from the perspective of theocentric ethics, obligatory because they flow from piety. Yet, to cite Gustafson's comment again, "one does not have to be willing to be damned for the glory of God to be moved to forms of self-giving toward others and restraint of individual and corporate interests . . . ."[18] Theocentric piety means self-denial for Gustafson, yet he specifically avoids advocating a form of denial so extreme that the balance between part and whole within communion is lost sight of. Gustafson by no means jettisons all love of self.

The Theology of the Cross

Religious ethics are generally mediated through cognitive symbols central to a particular tradition. In the Christian heritage, ethical ideals are mediated in part through the symbol of the cross. When the cross is understood as the final image of Christian perfection viewed as self-denial rather than as a means towards the end of redemptive communion, the meaning of Christian love is likely to be misconstrued. The cross, then, must be reconsidered in order that radical self-denial and love not be conflated.

In the writings of Samuel Hopkins, the cross is both the dominant symbol and the final expression of love. Consistently, Hopkins ignores the theology of nature and self-love characteristic of the Puritan Augustinians; in its place, Hopkins raises the image of the Christian crucified. In contrast to Hopkins, Edwards developed symbols of communion and mutual encounter; thus, the reciprocity between Father and Son within the trinity, as well as the mutual consent of being to being. In Edwards' theology, the cross, symbol of self-denying love, is surrounded by images of fellowship and union such that mutuality still remains the ideal form of Christian love.

Definitions of Christian love, then, are often dependent on particular understandings of the cross. This is as it must be, for the cross is perhaps the central symbol of Christian faith. Martin Luther King, Jr., for example, viewed the cross not as an end in itself but as a means by which community can be restored: "The cross is the eternal expression of the length to which God will go in order to restore broken community."[19] The correlative definition of Christian love offered by King is the following: "Agape is love seeking to preserve and create community."[20] King's insights into the essentially communal nature of Christian love doubtless developed out of his social philosophy of the self which stressed the interrelatedness of persons in mutual dependencies; yet the symbol of the cross and the meaning King attached to it provided him a source of crucial support for his doctrine of love. In contrast to King, the cross can be viewed as the chief good of Christian life and as itself the expression of the highest Christian idealism. No longer a means to the good of community, the cross is an end in itself. The correlative definition of Christian love is self-denial that is above all disinterested in response. The Mennonite theologian John Howard Yoder presents roughly this view with his claim that the Christian is to "accept the cross as his destiny, to move toward it and even provoke it . . . ."[21]

To correct those understandings of the cross which emphasize the total denial of self-love, consider first the possibility that Christ came to be loved as well as to love. If he had not hoped for a response to his love, then why did he cry out over Jerusalem before his crucifixion, using the metaphor of a hen longing to gather her brood under her wings? Is there not real pathos and tragedy here, comprehensive only if Christ <u>sought</u> the beloved community he could not find? Later, Christ was troubled by his three major disciples, who were unable to stay awake and pray with him at Gethsemane. Finally, he cried out from the cross, "Forgive them, for they know not what they do." These events indicate that Christ did not want his love to be rejected, but rather longed for the reciprocity upon which he could build community. That he had to go the extra mile through crucifixion does not discount the possibility that his love was motivated by a desire to be accepted and loved, i.e., by a certain form of self-love. As King writes, Christian love "goes the second mile <u>to restore community</u> (italics mine)." It forgives "seventy times seven <u>to restore community</u> "(italics mine) as well.[22]

One useful article on Christian love and the cross is that of Herbert Warren Richardson, in which he draws on King's thought. Richardson himself understands faith as "the power of reconciliation" which works to unite those in conflict. He appreciates King's thought because it includes a faith in the power of "divine unity working in all things to reconcile. . . ."[23] Richardson is also attracted to King because of the latter's stress on friendship as the ultimate value of human life and on the struggle against evil as a quest for total interrelatedness.[24] In particular, Richardson is critical of the "Reformation dogma, affirming that Christian live is self-sacrificing agape—not personal communion."[25] Self-sacrifice, suggests Richardson, is understood by King as something which "grows naturally out of the love of friendship."[26] His comments on self-sacrifice as a means to the end of restored communion correlate with a view of the meaning of the cross akin to that of King. But Richardson is more than a commentator on King's theology, for the emphasis on love as communion and the self at essentially social is social is a part of his previous work.[27]

In addition to King and Richardson, the interpretation of the cross offered by Daniel Day Williams is of great interest. Williams, a process thinker, begins with a discussion of love as revealed in the Old Testament. This is a love between God and Israel which is "given and received on both sides."[28] The language used to describe this love relationship is taken from the special relations found in the family, e.g., "love between father and son, and between husband and bride."[29] The Old Testament, then, does not have any difficulty with the notion of love as essentially mutual and joyful. Indeed, the entire history of Israel can be understood as God's repeated efforts to create opportunities for the voluntary restoration of community with humanity. That Israel often failed to seize these opportunities is cause for divine suffering and self-sacrifice.

Turning to the New Testament, Williams finds no discontinuity with the Old. "Agape," he writes, "is first and primordially the spirit of communion willing the divine relationship between Father and Son as the ground and pattern of the fulfillment of all things."[30] Williams, then, has no difficulty in placing friendship and reciprocity at the center of Christian ethics.

With regard to self-sacrifice and the cross, Williams comments that these are necessary "in the light of the need of man."[31]   Because humanity refuses to enter into communion with God, "God has to deal with a humanity which can learn to love and be reached only through the divine self-giving and suffering."[32]   The cross symbolizes this suffering and self-sacrifice, but these are hardly viewed as ends in themselves.   There is a tragic dimension to the cross, for it signifies divine suffering and agonizing over an unresponsive world.   God's love takes on a unilateral and sacrificial character, but this by no means displaces the essential core of love, which remains community.   As Williams puts it, "There is no sense in denying motivation to the actions of God any more than to the action of a human lover who desires reconciliation with another."[33]   For Williams, the cross does not capture the meaning of Christian love unless it is carefully interpreted within the wider context of mutuality and interpersonal communion.

The understanding of the cross in relation to Christian love exhibited in the writings of King, Richardson, and Williams has been a minority viewpoint among Protestants.   Reinhold Niebuhr, for instance, interpreted the cross as a symbol of judgment against all but an utterly disinterested and self-sacrificial love.   The emergence of feminist ethics has gradually forced the minority viewpoint into the center stage.   Valerie Saiving, for instance, argued that the Niebuhrian interpretation of Christian love is unsatisfactory from a feminist perspective, insofar as it denounces the normally acceptable forms of self-love that women have too often been denied.[34]   Building on Saiving's work, Barbara Andolsen maintains that the ideal of Christian love is community and mutuality rather than radical self-denial.[35]

What is most interesting about Andolsen's argument for the purposes of this discussion is her reliance on the notion that the crucifixion of Christ was not an act of self-immolation pursued for the sake of self-denial. Rather, the cross testifies to Christ's unswerving commitment to mutual love.[36] (Here, Andolsen draws on some writings of Beverly Harrison, unpublished at the time of her writing.[37])

There is an important conclusion to be drawn from this overview of the theme of love as community in contemporary Protestant ethics: the cross, if understood as an end in itself rather than a means to the restoration of communion, must be carefully reinterpreted. This means that Christian ethicists must go about the difficult task of rethinking the life of Christ in light of the crucifixion.

Recently, Catholic theologian and moralist Richard Westley has written the following controversial words:

> Suppose that the Jews had heard his call and the nation was converted. Suppose further that he therefore went out beyond Israel preaching the Good News of the Coming Kingdom.[38]

Westley refers here, of course, to Christ. His thesis is that the crucifixion was not necessary for salvation, despite the prevailing orthodoxy formalized through Anselm's Cur Deus Homo to the contrary. The cross, argues Westley, does not serve as a satisfactory symbol of "redemptive intimacy" and should therefore be understood as an indication of human unresponsiveness to divine longings. As Westley concludes, "Admittedly, salvation by crucifixion and immolation is one way to tell the story of our salvation. It is the thesis of this book that it is neither the best nor the only way to do so."[39] What Westley does is shift the discussion of Christian love away from the symbol

of the cross, at least as the cross has commonly been understood.

One of Westley's most interesting discussions focuses on the understanding of the cross in the early Christian church. He points out, with some substantive biblical scholarship to back him up, that the earliest church was uncertain about the meaning of the cross. After all, Stephen lashed out at the Jewish leaders for their stubborn refusal to follow Christ, and finally denounced them as murderers and betrayers. (Acts 7:53) Paul himself states that had the rulers of the time known, they would not have crucified the Lord of Glory. (I Cor. 2:8) Evidently some strains in the New Testament indicate that the early community did not achieve total consensus as to the necessity of the cross.

The rather radical reinterpretation of the cross which Westley develops may not ring true to orthodox Christian theologians, and perhaps it does go too far from inherited wisdom in certain respects. Nevertheless, it serves as a highly suggestive counterpoint that moves in a direction that, if taken seriously, can have major implications for future work on the theme of Christian love.

Indeed, Protestant ethics will have difficulty incorporating the ideals of true self-love and communion until a discussion of the meaning of the cross opens up. Gilbert C. Meilaender, for instance, writing out of the Lutheran tradition, has recently argued on behalf of friendship.[40] Philia, he maintains, characterized by mutuality and preference, ought to have a place in Protestant ethics. It is, writes Meilaender, important to develop a positive view of philia, for it is grounded in "the needs and possibilities of our human nature."[41] But alas, Meilaender's appreciation of friendship is rather limited because of his insistance that the ideal of Christian love must still be understood as "purely disinterested." Hovering high above "the needs and possibilities of our human nature" is the "divine agape" and with it "possibilities beyond those of our nature."[42] Thus, Meilaender cannot permit his _philia_ to move to the center of Christian ethics. There is an opposition—at least a tension—in his thought between the natural order of friendship and self-love in community and the supernatural order of utterly selfless love. Finally, his notion of Christian love is essentially self-denying rather than essentially personal communion. Were Meilaender to rethink in fundamental terms the meaning of the cross in the light of Christ's own divine longing for communion, the dualistic tension in his ethic might well be resolved.

There may be a rapproachment between Protestant and Catholic ethics on the horizon, one which defines Christian love in terms of true self-love in community. In addition to thinkers such as King, Richardson, and Williams, the recent writings of William F. May and James M. Gustafson emphasize love as communion also. Both were students of H. Richard Niebuhr, whose social philosophy of the self implies a mutual notion of love. May defines love as "continuing reciprocity of need" and Gustafson as freely giving and freely receiving.[43] Increasingly, the definition of Christian love as unilateral giving characteristic of Anders Nygren and Reinhold Niebuhr, once a dominant force, is on the wane. Protestant ethicists in the mainstream can now agree with the Catholic Martin D'Arcy that, "The simplest statement of the law which governs what is highest and lowest in the Universe can be that of 'Give and Take'."[44] They can agree as well with the Russian thinker Nicolas Berdyaev that, "The true purpose and meaning of love is not to . . . cultivate virtues which elevate the soul, or attain perfection, but to reach the union of souls, fellowship, and brotherhood."[45] Christian love is being understood as a two-term relation presupposing the meeting of lovers in communion and unity.

What, then, of self-denial? It may increasingly be understood as the natural overflow of joyful communion, for those in communion and unity give to one another freely. Alas, when relationships require restoration, sacrificial love will be needed to create fellowship. But self-denial need not be seen as an end in itself. The negative definition of love as simply self-denying, unmotivated, self-crucifying, and so forth is giving way to a new consensus, for which the essence of love is, in the memorable words of Daniel Day Williams, "seeking the enjoyment of freedom in communion with the other."[46]

The Human Fault

Ann Douglas has carefully detailed the use to which the Congregationalist clergy put their doctrine of disinterested benevolence. Generally, it was used by men to control women. Douglas, a feminist historian of American religion and culture, cites Horace Bushnell's letter to his daughter, written in 1845, instructing her that women make the best Christians because they have no needs of their own, and exist solely "for the world's comfort."[47] The lesson to be learned here is that radical self-denial emerging from religious experience can create social chaos and injustice when it carries over into the sphere of human interrelations.

For Samuel Hopkins, "sin" or the human fault was identified with all forms of self-love. He saw this "sin" operative in Newport society with its slave trade and avarice. The antithesis of this "sin" is complete self-denying love, and Hopkins, as to be expected, articulated this. Self-love, he insisted, is nothing more than a "wild beast." Perhaps because Edwards had not been exposed to the havoc of Yankee mercantilism as was Hopkins, he had a more tolerant view of one understanding of self-love than did his student. Thus, while Edwards had no patience with selfishness, he did not spin the dubious ideal of selflessness from the genuine virtue of unselfishness. This transformation awaited Hopkins, who made of selflessness a holy image of perfection. Edwards maintained a sense of proportionality between all the parts of the whole, and looked askance at any ethic insisting that a particular part no longer be included within that whole.

American feminist theologian and ethicist Valerie Saiving has stated the unsatisfactory aspects of what amounts to the Hopkinsian notion of "sin." Because feminists have pointed out the morally problematic dimensions of "disinterested benevolence" with regard to nineteenth-century American women, it is fitting that I make use of Saiving at this juncture.

Saiving is especially critical of the writings of Anders Nygren and Reinhold Niebuhr, for they confuse the particulars of male experience with the universal. The modern West, with its emphasis on "laissez-faire competition and economic uncertainty," has set free "precisely those aspects of human nature which are peculiarly significant to men."[48] The theology of Nygren and Niebuhr addresses this dimension of masculine experience in the modern world. However, insists Saiving, feminine "sin" is distinct from masculine. Women sin through the "negation of self," lacking self-definition and clear identity. The antithesis of feminine "sin" is certainly not selfless love and radical self-denial, but rather a fitting affirmation of self within the community of being.[49]

What thinkers such as Douglas and Saiving underscore is the tragic consequence of the ideal of disinterestedness for women. It appears that "disinterested benevolence" has been used for manipulative purposes as well as for good, and this ambiguity highlights the Achilles' heel of the concept, at least as Hopkins defined it. When the ideal of radical self-denial spills over into the social sphere, it gives the neighbor what Gene Outka refers to as a "blank check."[50] Because the Christian has no grounds upon which to assert limits to self-giving, the likely result is what the feminists refer to as "the experience of nothingness." By this they mean a state of utter immolation and self-disolution brought about by an ideal of seeking only the good of the order.

The confusion, then, over the nature of the human fault is a significant one. Edwards, by emphasizing unselfishness without moving towards selflessness, provides Christian ethics with a response to the forms of manipulation against which feminist theologians complain.

Christian Love: Positive and Negative Definitions

One of Edwards' great contributions to American theological ethics is his positive definition of Christian love. By "positive" I mean, for lack of a better word, "upbeat." His thoughts on love are an upward stroke, lively and inspirational. The consent of being to being of which he wrote points in the direction of full communion and mutual well-being, akin in the American tradition to Royce's "beloved community." Hopkins, contrary to Edwards, allows only a negative definition of Christian love. Love is associated with a "willingness to be damned" and an austere denial of self.

A   contemporary   theologian,   Joseph

Haroutunian, has carefully defined the limits of such negative definitions: ". . . the definition of love in negatives as 'unconditional, uncaused, unmotivated, groundless, uncalculating'; as self-giving, self-denying, self-crucifying, simply outgoing; as unprudential, unevaluating, unteleogical , etc., leave us with a 'love' that is not only impossible for human beings, regenerate or unregenerate, but also of doubtful Biblical and theological validity."[51] Haroutunian has in mind Anders Nygren and Reinhold Niebuhr here, both of them decidedly negative in their descriptions of Christian love. I think Haroutunian's viewpoint is a valuable one, insofar as it highlights the somewhat morbid tone of the negative definitions. One wonders how it is that any human being can have the moral resources to abide by the terms of such a self-renouncing ideal.

Edwards was able to avoid the quagmire of negative definition in part because he feared melancholy and therefore sought to restrain gloomy terminology. Thus the language of God's "sweetness, " of "perfect reciprocity" and so forth. In addition, and more importantly for Christian ethical theory, Edwards developed his notion of virtue for embodied life experience. Edwards took seriously the emotional inclinations of human beings, and recognized that moral idealism must be grounded in the affections of the heart. Because one rationally wills the good does not mean that one will be able to act well, for at the deepest levels of human experience lie the affections, and these provide the self with a basic orientation more basic than will itself. As Richard R. Niebuhr has written, "A true affection lies as such a depth in personal existence that it is inaccessible to volition. So much is clear from the fact that it is affection that endows the will with its specific tone and energy."[52] Edwards was concerned with making the duty of Christian love emotionally satisfying; that is, how to make it flow from inclination, and not merely a matter of arid self-denial and the austere sense of doing one's duty for its own sake. He understood that affection lies at the core of moral, as well as Christian, life. In short, he was unwilling to separate head and heart. Edwards found the dreary, even chilling language of Hopkins both emotionally burdensome and destructive of virtue's spontaneity. Thus, Edwards simply could not condone the Hopkinsian test of "the willingness to be damned," for such a test makes demands contrary to affectional inclination. One acts out of duty to the glory of God in Hopkins' system, with no attention given to the emotional center of experience.

Those contemporary American theologians inspired by Edwards' thought tend to have rather positive definitions of Christian love. Thus, H. Richard Niebuhr writes as follows:

> By love we mean at least these attitudes and actions: rejoicing in the presence of the beloved, gratitude, reverence and loyalty toward him. Love is rejoicing over the existence of the beloved one; it is the desire that he be rather than not be; it is longing for his presence when he is absent; it is happiness in the thought of him; it is profound satisfaction over everything that makes him great and glorious. Love is gratitude: it is thankfulness for the existence of the beloved; it is the happy acceptance of everything that he gives without the jealous feeling that the self ought to be able to do as much; it is gratitude that does not seek equality; it is wonder over the other's gift of himself in companionship.[53]

Of course Niebuhr takes self-sacrifice for the other into account, acknowledging that the loyalty love demands may require the supreme sacrifice. But overall, the language used here is positive and inspirational. Rejoice in love, long for the beloved, be happy in the thought of the neighbor, and love with a feeling of profound satisfaction. James M. Gustafson quotes the above definition in its full, for he considers it "one of the finest statements of the meaning of love in theological literature."[54] In tone it is Edwardsean, capturing in detail the meaning of affectional consent of being to being.

Theological Anthropology

Theological anthropology plays a major role in determining the position any given theologian takes regarding the meaning of Christian love. The disparity between Edwards and Hopkins is pronounced with regard to the anthropological question. On the one hand, Edwards understood the Christian in terms of two distinct principles, the "natural" and the "divine." The "natural principle" consist of self-love, i.e., the natural concern for one's own well-being and happiness; the "divine principle," a gift of grace, is beyond self-love. In the language of classical theology, Edwards distinguishes between what can be called the imago Dei and the "likeness" or similitude of God. As James M. Childs writes, "the union of the body and the soul is understood as constituting man's natural makeup in the image of God. The likeness or similitude, which perfect man also possesses, is a product of the outpouring of the Spirit in man's spirit."[55] Edwards' anthropology is dichotomous in structure, retaining natural inclination and affection in the image of the regenerate Christian. Hopkins, however, rejected this structure of dichotomy, opting for a structural monism.

Thus, in Miscellany 301, Edwards writes of the "natural and necessary inclination that man has to his own benefit." The human fault is not the presence of such inclination, but rather its breaking out "into all manner of exorbitancies."[56] The saint aims at happiness, but in a way subordinate to the glory of God. In another miscellany, Edwards argues that "The more a man loves God, the more unwilling will he be to be deprived of happiness."[57] Throughout his corpus, Edwards does not seek to extinguish the natural self, but rather to subordinate it. Because the "natural principle" is retained, Edwards cannot take the position that Christian love consists of radical self-denial to the extent that the desire for happiness and true well-being is ignored. For Edwards, the desires and inclinations of nature play a significant role in the theology of love. To the end, Edwards held that "It is not a thing contrary to Christianity that a man should love himself, or, which is the same thing, should love his own happiness."[58]

Samuel Hopkins, on the other hand, ignores the limits which the natural principle of self-love places on self-denial. There is no structural dichotomy in his thought regarding the regenerate, for all that is natural has been swept aside without compromise. Specifically, the inclinations of the natural self are "not only no part of holiness, but opposed to it." However much self-love can be restrained, it is still self-love, and therefore the opposite of holiness. This anthropological monism allows Hopkins to take piety of utter resignation seriously whereas Edwards could not.

What is at stake in the debate between Edwards and Hopkins is the perennial question of the degree to which any theology of love must take into account the structures of individual human nature. Edwards, taking his direction from the Augustinian tradition, did not see Christian love and proper self-love as contradictory. He was in agreement with Samuel Willard and others—God works with human nature, rather than against it. I think there is wisdom in Edwards' thought on this point, for why suppose that God has not created human nature as a good? To be moved by the Spirit is not necessarily to be impelled to self-immolation.

Love and the Social Self

Jonathan Edwards' empiricism allowed him to take the "natural principle" of the self into theological account; it also permitted him to observe the thoroughly social character of human existence. The consent of being to being as well as perfected reciprocity in heaven and within the deity indicate how important the sociality of human life was to him. To refuse this sociality meant nothing less than a refusal of human experience. Edwards' limits on self-denial are in part, then, grounded in his philosophy of the self, for in the extreme, such denial can mean the refusal of participation in the mutual good.

Those contemporary theologians influenced by Edwards place high value on his view of the social self. H. Richard Niebuhr, however much he was informed by the thought of Josiah Royce, George Herbert Mead, and Martin Buber, was also deeply moved by Edwards' emphasis on social interrelations. Consent of being to being meant, for Niebuhr, an image of "the social character of all human life."[59] "To be a self," he writes, "in the presence of other selves is not a derivative experience but primordial."[60] The self "comes to knowledge of itself in the presence of other selves."[61] There is no solitary self, for such individualism is largely illusion. Niebuhr reached these sorts of conclusions with the help of social scientists like Mead and Harry Stack Sullivan, empiricists all; and in Edwards, he discovered these conclusions as well.

Given this philosophy of the self, Niebuhr, like

Edwards, has some sense of the limits of self-denial. In one class lecture, he specifically disputed the ideal of radical self-denial as follows (cited by James Fowler): "This does not mean the negation of the self, but the acceptance of the limitations upon the self, whereby others are being affirmed."[62] Self-denial in the context of theocentric piety "may force a man from his egocentricity," as it should, for God, not the self, is the proper center of all things."[63] To be forced from egocentricity, however, is not to give up the integrity of the self. Moreover, to transcend this preoccupation with self is not to become free of essential dependencies on others.

Some Americans theological ethicists have unfortunately been lured away from the proposition that, as Buber argues, "We live our lives inscrutably included within the streaming mutual life of the universe."[64] This has been due in large part to the influence of Kierkegaard. Kierkegaard has a markedly unrealistic view of the self as a "single one," free of all essential relationships, and beyond both need love and despair. Standing above "the crowd" Kierkegaard lived as well as he could in virtual isolation—he had no spouse and disdained friendship. In short, Kierkegaard failed to accomplish the ideal of love as communion in every sphere of his life. Having refused participation in the mutual good of communion, Kierkegaard glorifies a thoroughly unilateral form of love rooted in the determination of the will rather than affection. He manages to arrive at a test for the selfless purity of Christian love as follows: "If one wants to make sure that love is completely unselfish he eliminates every possibility of repayment. But precisely this is what is eliminated in love for the dead."[65] This strikes me as a dubious test, designed to drive a thick wedge between all self-love and Christian love characteristic of those theologians who cannot acknowledge the good of reciprocity.

109

What sort of image of fulfillment does Kierkegaard provide? In fact, fulfillment is a virtual impossibility in his system. As Buber points out in his essay entitled, "The Question of the Single One," Kierkegaard provides us with nothing but a "religious doctrine of loneliness." Kierkegaard at last made the confession that he "ceased to have common speech with others," having "nothing more to do with the world."[66] Because he refused to receive love in the "We" of relationship, finally he could love no more. The eclipse of love resulted from his moving outside the stream of mutually supportive experience. Kierkegaard's case underscores the futility of radically self-denying love. His claim that the only worthy form of Christian love is "sacrificial disinterestedness" was, in the last analysis, unsatisfactory to lived experience.

One of the more widely read books on Christian love of recent has been Gene Outka's Agape: An Ethical Analysis. Outka is to be praised for placing careful limits on self-sacrifice for the neighbor. However, his book is problematic because of its heavy indebtedness to Kierkegaard. Christian love as mutuality and communion is specifically rejected. Instead, agape is defined in terms of "equal regard for the neighbor" which transcends peculiar idiosyncrasies. The neighbor is to be love dutifully qua human existent, and for no other reasons. In arguing this, Outka consistently makes reference to Kierkegaard's Works of Love.[67] Indeed, Outka highlights Kierkegaard's claim that self-love has a place only in preferential relations, while "self-renunciation" is the essence of neighbor-regard.[68] It is quite true that Outka brings to his analysis Kierkegaard's concerns about "misplaced caressing indulgence" and other possible strategic limits to self-renunciation, but the ultimate meaning of Christian love for Outka is still a unilateral and essentially self-sacrificial one which devalues the ideal of communion. Granted, Outka tries to distinguish love as self-sacrifice from love as neighbor-regard, but this distinction is at best a fragile one. If we move back to Paul Ramsey's statement that there are "two main interpretations of the meaning of Christian love," i.e., self-sacrifice or communion, it is clear where Outka (and Kierkegaard) lies.

Outka, then, falls victim to Kierkegaard's individualism. There is little or no appreciation in his work for the ideal of deeply and freely receptive and responsive communion. There is no sense of the "beauty" of mutual consent such that each part responds richly to every other part. We are left with an atomic exclusiveness which still leaves both lover and beloved in separation. Had Outka taken Edwards into account, the inadequacies of his view of the human self might have been mitigated. "Love in heaven," wrote Edwards, "is always mutual."[69]

Final Reflections

The ideal of Christian love which I defend is one defined by complete and continual exchange as well as affirmation, a perfect interaction and communion, inclusive of true self-love. Participation in the mutual good is the irreplaceable basis of moral growth. Granted, Christian love does assume the posture of radical self-denial when the circular flow of give and take is interrupted; yet finally, the true meaning of love is not the cultivation of disinterestedness. There is sublime beauty in the harmony and joy of communion which simply cannot be dismissed as sub-Christian. The word "religion" itself, it is often said, comes from the Latin "ligare," i.e., it means to be "bound" anew in communion. The basis of Christian ethics can be nothing other than complete reciprocity.

Those who would devalue this ideal generally begin by denying the Christian significance of true self-love—the only love worthy of the Christian is an indifferent gift-love, they claim. If the Christian transcends all love of self, then the ideal of communion is undercut completely, for what is communion if not the reciprocal meeting of needs and wants? The transcending of all self-love is only possible if the last vestige of inclination and desire is driven from the self. Consequently, myriad Christians have attempted just this: the medieval pure love mystics tried to annihilate self totally, such that in loving God they were not seeking God as were the Augustinians; this ideal of selfless love passed over into the American theological tradition creating a powerful current of thought which finally led to the notion of a love for the neighbor so fully disinterested as to violate the structure of personal and social human nature; and American thinkers from Edwards to Royce to Williams have sought to retrieve the meaning of communion and love of self for our ethical tradition. The contemporary American controversy over the meaning of Christian love is still colored by the Edwards-Hopkins divergence as it was bequeathed to the Nineteenth Century and examined by modern ethicists sensitive to the history of American Protestant ideas. All to often, it is assumed that the Protestant evangelical tradition is not the divided house that it is with regard to the love theme. Hopefully I have dispelled this assumption, and pointed out the relative merit of the ideas which Edwards set in motion. Edwards' fundamental contribution to American thought lies in his insistence that the part be related essentially to the whole of community, rather than detached in a posture of an all too radical ethic of self-denial.

Footnotes

1. Paul Ramsey, <u>Nine Modern Moralists</u> (Lanham, Md.: University Press of America, 1983), p. 131.

2. <u>Ibid.</u>

3. <u>Ibid.</u>, p. 133.

4. William A. Sadler, <u>Existence and Love</u> (New York: Scribners, 1969), p. 212.

5. Jonathan Edwards, <u>Charity and Its Fruits</u> (London: Banner of Truth Press, 1978), p. 338.

6. <u>Ibid.</u>

7. <u>Ibid.</u>, p. 339.

8. <u>Ibid.</u>, p. 347.

9. Rudolf Otto, <u>The Idea of the Holy</u> (London: Oxford University Press, 1980), p. 50.

10. Evelyn Underhill, <u>Mysticism</u> (New York: Dutton, 1978), p. 164, n. 3.

11. Paul Ramsey, <u>Basic Christian Ethics</u> (Chicago: University of Chicago Midway Reprint, 1978), p. 151.

12. <u>Ibid.</u>

13. <u>Ibid.</u>

14. Reinhold Niebuhr, <u>Moral Man and Immoral Society</u> (New York: Scribner's, 1932), pp. 55-56.

15. Walter Rauschenbusch, <u>The Righteousness of the Kingdom</u>, ed. Max L. Stackhouse (Nashville: Abington Press, 1968), p. 263.

16. Joasiah Royce, <u>The Problem of Christianity</u> (Chicago: University of Chicago Press, 1984), p. 88.

17. James M. Gustafson, <u>Ethics From a Theocentric Perspective</u> (Chicago: University of Chicago Press, 1984), vol. 2:22.

18. <u>Ibid.</u>

19. Martin Luther King, Jr., in James M. Washington, ed., <u>A Testament of Hope: The Essential Writings of Martin Luther King, Jr.</u> (San Francisco: Harper & Row, 1986), p. 20.

20. <u>Ibid.</u>

21. John Howard Yoder, <u>The Politics of Jesus</u> (Grand Rapids: Wm. B. Eerdmans, Co., 1972), p. 132.

22. King, <u>op. cit.</u>, p. 20.

23. Herbert Warren Richardson, "Martin Luther King—Unsung Theologian", in Martin E. Marty and Dean G. Peerman, eds., <u>New Theology No. 6</u> (New York: Macmillan, 1969). p. 180.

24. <u>Ibid.</u>, p. 183.

25. <u>Ibid.</u>

26. <u>Ibid.</u>

27. Richardson, <u>Toward an American Theology</u> (New York: Harper & Row, 1966).

28. Daniel Day Williams, <u>The Spirit and Forms of Love</u> (Lanham, Md,: University Press of America, 1981), p. 20.

29. Ibid., p. 19.

30. Ibid., p. 37.

31. Ibid., p. 38.

32. Ibid., p. 37.

33. Ibid., p. 38.

34. Valerie Saiving, "The Human Situation: A Feminine View," in Womenspirit Rising, ed. Carol Christ and Judith Plaskow (New York: Harper, 1979), pp. 25-42.

35. Barbara Hilkert Andolsen, "Agape in Feminist Ethics," Journal of Religious Ethics, vol. 9/1, Spring, 1981.

36. Ibid., p. 78

37. Beverly Harrison is best known for her work on abortion, some of which reflects concern that self-denial and womanhood not be tied together.

38. Richard Westley, Redemptive Intimacy (Mystic, Ct.: Twenty-Third Publications, 1981), p. 115.

39. Ibid., p. 116.

40. Gilbert C. Meilaender, Friendship: A Study in Theological Ethics (Notre Dame: University of Notre Dame Press, 1981).

41. Ibid., p. 105.

42. Ibid.

43. William F. May, "Code, Covenant, Contract, or Philanthrophy," Hastings Center Report 5

(December, 1975), p. 32; also, James M. Gustafson, Ethics From a Theocentric Prespective (Chicago: University of Chicago Press, 1984), vol. 2, pp. 161-165.

44. Martin C. D'Arcy, The Mind and Heart of Love (Cleveland: World Publishing Co., 1967), p. 14.

45. Nicolas Berdyaev, The Destiny of Man (London: Geoffrey Bliss, 1937), p. 187.

46. Daniel Day Williams, op. cit., p. 3.

47. Ann Douglas, The Feminization of American Culture (New York: Avon Books, 1977), p. 50.

48. Valerie Saiving, op. cit., p. 35.

49. Ibid., p. 38.

50. See Gene Outka, Agape: An Ethical Analysis (New Haven: Yale University Press, 1972), ch. 1.

51. Joseph Haroutunian, God With Us (Philadelphia: Westminster Press, 1965), p. 207.

52. Richard R. Niebuhr, Experiential Religion (New York: Harper & Row, 1972), p. 46.

53. H. Richard Niebuhr, with James M. Gustafson and Daniel Day Williams, The Purpose of the Church and Its Ministry (New York: Harper & Row, 1956), p. 55.

54. James M. Gustafson, Ethics From a Theocentric Perspective, vol. 2, p. 169, n. 7.

55. James M. Childs, Jr., Christian Anthropology and Ethics (Philadelphia: Fortress Press, 1978), p. 19.

56. Jonathan Edwards, "Miscellany 301" in The Philosophy of Jonathan Edwards, ed. Harvey G. Townsend (Eugene, Oregon: University of Oregon Press, 1955), pp. 242-243.

57. Edwards, "Miscellany 530" in The Philosophy of Jonathan Edwards, p. 202.

58. Ibid.

59. H. Richard Niebuhr, The Responsible Self (New York: Harper & Row, 1963), p. 69.

60. Ibid.

61. Ibid.

62. H. Richard Niebuhr as cited by James Fowler in To See the Kingdom (Nashville: Abington Press, 1974), pp. 196-197.

63. Ibid.

64. Martin Buber, I and Thou, trans. R. G. Smith (New York: Charles Scribner's Sons, 1958), p. 16.

65. Soren Kierkegaard, Works of Love, trans. Howard and Edna Hong (New York: Harper & Row, 1962), p. 320.

66. Martin Buber, Between Man and Man (New York: Macmillan, 1965), p. 55.

67. Gene Outka, op. cit., ch. 1.

68. Ibid.

69. Jonathan Edwards, Charity and Its Fruits, p. 338.

Index

120